SECOND EDITION

English Across the Curriculum

Content-area Vocabulary and Skills

TEACHER'S MANUAL

For Books 1, 2, and 3

Margaret Martin Maggs

National Textbook Company
a division of *NTC Publishing Group* • Lincolnwood, Illinois USA

Published by National Textbook Company, a division of NTC Publishing Group.
© 1993 by NTC Publishing Group, 4255 West Touhy Avenue,
Lincolnwood (Chicago), Illinois 60646-1975 USA.

2 3 4 5 6 7 8 9 0 VP 9 8 7 6 5 4 3 2 1

CONTENTS

INTRODUCTION

English Across the Curriculum is a series of three books designed especially for limited English proficient students. The series presents vocabulary in context and provides practice exercises in the basic skills necessary for success in academic subjects. The purpose of this material is to give ESL students opportunities to review and reinforce content-area information while learning the English language. *English Across the Curriculum* can be used by ESL teachers as well as subject-area teachers who are not trained in ESL techniques but who have limited English proficient students in their classrooms. Bilingual teachers will find the series useful for reinforcement lessons after teaching in the native language.

The books are arranged sequentially in terms of difficulty for the limited English proficient learner. Book 1 presents basic school vocabulary, such as classroom directions, subject names, and vocabulary related to specific subject areas. Book 2 expands student knowledge of basic reference materials (the dictionary, the encyclopedia, indexes, tables of contents, directories, schedules, diagrams). It promotes the skills students need for test-taking, report writing, organizing and studying. Book 3 provides more advanced study skills lessons in using the dictionary, categorizing, understanding relationships, synthesizing, predicting, and judging fact vs. opinion. Also included are cause and effect determinations; specialized reading of advertising, mood, and figurative language; and specialized algebraic, science, and computer vocabulary.

Those who have used *English Across the Curriculum* will note several changes that have been made to update the series for this second edition. Computer vocabulary replaces that of Home Ec and Shop. In Book 1 each group of exercises has been expanded with an "Ask a Friend" activity to encourage cooperation and language production. The test-taking lessons in Book 2 include material on standardized test forms. The order of some lessons has been changed, for example "Studying for Tests" now follows the test-taking to facilitate comprehension and reinforce skills on lessons.

General Suggestions for Use by non-ESL Content-Area Teachers

If you have students in your classroom who are learning English, you will find these books particularly helpful. You cannot, of course, simply hand the books to your students and expect them to learn. It is always best to precede any work in the book with an oral presentation and practice session. You may not have enough time to work individually with your ESL student; in that case you can assign another student to help. The following steps will enhance the learning situation:

1. Sit with the student and preview the material to be learned.

2. Pronounce new vocabulary clearly while pointing to the words and pictures used. Pronounce each word twice, then have the student repeat it at least twice.

3. Ask the student to read the explanatory material in the lesson aloud. If there is something in the classroom to reinforce learning (a dictionary, a written report on the board), use that to expand understanding. Answer any questions the student may have.

4. Go over exercise instructions with the student to make sure they are understood.

5. Have the student do the exercises and check them. Where there are errors, correct them promptly.

6. Do any of the additional activities suggested for the specific lesson.

    Social Studies Vocabulary Lessons: Book 1, Lessons 3, 9, 13

    Math Vocabulary Lessons: Book 1, Lessons 4, 10, 14, 15

    Science Vocabulary Lessons: Book 1, Lessons 5, 11

    English Language Arts Vocabulary Lessons: Book 1, Lessons 6, 12

    Computer Vocabulary Lesson: Book 1, Lesson 8

    Art/Music Vocabulary Lesson: Book 1, Lesson 7

General Suggestions for Use by ESL Teachers

This series is an adjunct to your ESL course. You will find it useful in a number of ways.

1. Book 1 is a basic vocabulary book that can supplement your regular vocabulary teaching with its specialized school vocabulary. Syntax is intentionally kept very simple so that lessons can fit easily into whatever structures you are currently teaching.

2. Books 2 and 3 are a ready source of reading and writing materials for the beginning to intermediate class. Since they provide a wide variety of exercises, they can be adapted to almost any ESL course that is preparing students who must soon enter or who are already in mainstream classes.

3. The series may serve as the text for a separate course within an ESL sequence of courses, particularly at the secondary level where students may be taking two or more hours of ESL daily. In this case, the series is particularly useful since it begins at the simplest level for the student who literally knows no English and advances to the level of the student who may be receiving most or all of his/her subject area instruction in English.

4. The series may serve as a resource for the ESL teacher who is working as a "pull-out" teacher for those programs which do not offer whole-class ESL instruction. The ESL teacher can use this series to aid the student who spends most of the day unassisted in a totally English-language learning environment.

5. For the ESL teacher who wishes to interpolate this series with the ongoing traditional course, there are specific suggestions listed for each lesson.

Cooperative Learning

Learning activities in which pairs or groups of students focus cooperatively on a task can be of great use in teaching limited English proficient students. Such activities encourage oral language production. They release the teacher from the responsibility of dominating an entire classroom and allow her or him to move around the room and observe individual student learning more closely. For the very beginning student, Book 1 offers cooperative learning activities entitled "Ask a Friend." For more advanced students, many of the suggested activities for lessons in Books 2 and 3 can easily be accomplished by pairs or groups of students.

If you are a non-ESL content-area teacher, you will probably have best results when you pair an English-dominant student with the English-language learner. Be sure to vary the choice of student from lesson to lesson so that the ESL learner has the opportunity to produce and react to different language users. If this is not possible and you must pair ESL students together make sure that they understand that each one should take a turn asking the suggested questions. If absolutely necessary, you yourself may be the learner's "friend." Any of these suggested pairings will profit the student's ability to speak and understand English.

If you are an ESL teacher, you are probably already familiar with the techniques of cooperative learning. Any of the above groupings can be used, but be careful that you vary students for better social interactions and language development.

Testing

Evaluation tests are included in this manual in a separate section beginning on page 6. They can be used as informal placement tests or inventories. They can also be used for post-lesson evaluations. There is one test for Book 1; its five sections may be given separately by content area teachers. It may also be given as one complete test. In Books 2 and 3 there are two tests for each level.

Contents and Objectives

8 **Subject:** Art/Music

    Objective: Learning vocabulary: *paint, picture, draw, crayon, color, tape, piano, play, sing, song*

    Reinforcement: *Sometimes/many; What does* (noun) *do?* (Noun) verb + s

9 **Subject:** Social Studies

    Objective: Learning vocabulary: *direction, north, south, east, west, road, highway, bridge, lake, building*

    Reinforcement: Tag: *too;* quantities: *some/many*

10 **Subject:** Math

    Objective: Learning vocabulary: *plus, minus, equal, greater than, less than, total, fraction, whole, decimal, percent*

    Reinforcement: Comparatives: *more/less/greater than;* dependent clauses: *when we +* verb

11 **Subject:** Science

    Objective: Learning vocabulary: *flower, grow, season, weather, rain, temperature, up, hot, down, cold*

    Reinforcement: Contrasts: *up/down, hot/cold*

12 **Subject:** English

    Objective: Learning punctuation vocabulary: *punctuation, period, letter, capital, small, comma, question mark, date, signature*

    Reinforcement: Capitalization; letter writing

13 **Subject:** Social Studies

    Objective: Learning U.S. geographical vocabulary: *Northeastern, Mid-Atlantic, Southern, states, Midwestern, Southwestern, Western*

    Reinforcement: Spelling and capitalization of state names

14 **Subject:** Math

    Objective: Learning to read Math addition and subtraction word problems

    Reinforcement: Written cardinal numbers; *how many?*

15 **Subject:** Math

    Objective: Learning to read Math multiplication and division word problems

    Reinforcement: Oral numbers practice with multiplication tables

BOOK 2

1 **Subject:** Alphabetical order

    Objective: Learning to alphabetize by one and then two letters

    Reinforcement: Alphabetizing known words

2 **Subject:** The Library

    Objective: Learning about the library and vocabulary: *alphabetical order, reference, catalog, card, subject, title, author, dictionary, encylopedia, biography, fiction, nonfiction*

    Reinforcement: Visiting school / local library

3 Subject: The Dictionary / The Encyclopedia

Objective: Learning to use reference books

Reinforcement: Using a dictionary, encyclopedia

4 Subject: The Table of Contents / The Index

Objective: Learning to locate information in a book

Reinforcement: Practice with actual subject books

5 Subject: The Newspaper Index / The Telephone Directory

Objective: Learning to locate information in everyday references

Reinforcement: Practice with local newspaper, telephone directory

6 Subject: Schedules

Objective: Learning how to read various schedules

Reinforcement: Reading schedules from newspapers, airport television terminals, and bus and train publications

7 Subject: Diagrams

Objective: Learning how to read line drawings: box diagrams, line charts, bar charts and pie charts

Reinforcement: Drawing examples of diagrams and charts based on familiar information

8 Subject: Acquiring skills for academic success

Objective: Learning how to approach homework, how to complete standardized answer forms

Reinforcement: Practice homework assignments, practice completing forms

9 Subject: Test taking

Objective: Learning to take matching and missing word(s) tests

Reinforcement: Practice tests in various subject areas

10 Subject: Studying

Objective: Learning to study and memorize

Reinforcement: Practice assignments in studying and memorizing

11 Subject: Writing reports

Objective: Learning to write compositions and book reports

Reinforcement: Writing compositions and book reports

12 Subject: Writing reports

Objective: Learning to get information for reports

Reinforcement: Writing actual reports

13 Subject: The Outline / The Summary

Objective: Learning to organize and summarize information

Reinforcement: Preparing outlines and summaries

14	Subject:	Reading quickly
	Objective:	Learning how to locate important words in reading; learning how to read groups of words together
	Reinforcement:	Reading subject area books for information

15	Subject:	Judging important information
	Objective:	Learning to decide which information is important
	Reinforcement:	Practice with subject area books

BOOK 3

1	Subject:	Reading dictionary definitions
	Objective:	Understanding multiple definitions, synonyms, antonyms
	Reinforcement:	Understanding definitions of known multiple-meaning words, and their synonyms and antonyms

2	Subject:	Dictionary pronunciation
	Objective:	Understanding key word examples and accents
	Reinforcement:	Understanding dictionary key words and accents

3	Subject:	Categorizing
	Objective:	Practice organizing information into categories
	Reinforcement:	Categorizing with known vocabulary

4	Subject:	Understanding relationships
	Objective:	Understanding analogies of synonyms and numbers
	Reinforcement:	Writing analogies of synonyms and numbers

5	Subject:	Understanding relationships
	Objective:	Understanding analogies of antonyms and part to whole
	Reinforcement:	Writing analogies of antonyms and part to whole

6	Subject:	Putting facts together
	Objective:	Synthesizing and concluding from facts
	Reinforcement:	Combining and restating sentences

7	Subject:	Predicting
	Objective:	Learning to predict the next sentence or sentences
	Reinforcement:	Reading short stories and predicting the ending

8	Subject:	Predicting
	Objective:	Learning to predict the end of factual or fictional writing
	Reinforcement:	Writing open-ended short stories

9 **Subject:** Facts and Opinions

  Objective: Learning how to judge reading material for facts

  Reinforcement: Discovering fact and opinion sentences in reading

10 **Subject:** Cause and Effect

  Objective: Learning how to determine cause and effect in reading

  Reinforcement: Combining sentences that include cause and effect

11 **Subject:** Understanding hidden meaning

  Objective: Understanding implications in reading

  Reinforcement: Writing paragraphs that imply information or opinion

12 **Subject:** Mood and advertising

  Objective: Understanding implications of mood writing and/or advertising

  Reinforcement: Analyzing local advertising in newspapers and on television

13 **Subject:** Algebraic Vocabulary and Science Experiment Vocabulary

  Objective: Vocabulary: *numeral, constant, variable, phrase, expression, Bunsen burner, petri dish, test tube, slide, solution, emulsion, sterile, stain*

  Reinforcement: Using student texts and materials to clarify vocabulary

14 **Subject:** Computer vocabulary

  Objective: Vocabulary: *menu, cursor, mouse, function, pen, data, input, output, graphics, prompt, modem*

  Reinforcement: Using computer to clarify vocabulary

15 **Subject:** Figurative and humorous meanings

  Objective: Understanding and interpreting figurative and exaggerated comparisons

  Reinforcement: Writing examples of figurative or exaggerated comparisons

Informal Evaluation/Placement Tests

Scoring

Each test is worth 100 points. The test for Book 1 may be administered as five separate parts or as a whole. All tests indicate the number of points to be allotted each section and sub-section.

As with any test, reassure students that you are not out to trap them. Emphasize that these tests will make the best use of their time by building on what they know. Students with low scores should be congratulated for what they do know. You may want to withhold actual number scores and simply indicate level.

Evaluation Testing

Each test can be used for broad or pinpoint evaluation. For broad evaluation of student mastery, use the total points correct. Students should probably score at least 70 to indicate their broad mastery of the vocabulary and/or skills covered. For pinpoint evaluation, check errors to see if patterns emerge. Each section of the test is labeled to facilitate identification of areas that need reinforcement.

Placement Testing

Each test covers approximately half of a level. If you are not sure where a new student should be placed, try that student with a test you judge to be too easy for him or her. If the student achieves 90 or better, give the next test. If a student falls below 70 on a test, you will probably want that student to cover the level entirely.

BOOK 1	TEST

$$1, 2, 3, 4, 5, 6, 7, 8, 9, 10$$

$$444 - 123 = 321 \qquad \begin{array}{r} 77 \\ -16 \\ \hline 61 \end{array}$$

Math Learning
(20 points)

1. We study _____ .

    numbers   add   multiply

2. What do we do in Math?

    We _____ numbers.

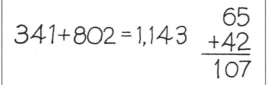

$$341 + 802 = 1,143 \qquad \begin{array}{r} 65 \\ +42 \\ \hline 107 \end{array}$$

3. We _____ numbers.

   add   subtract   multiply

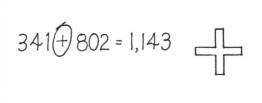

$$22 \times 2 = 44 \quad 5 \times 5 = 25$$
$$5 \cdot 5 = 25$$

4. What are these?

   They're _____ problems.

$$2 \div 2 = 1 \quad 10 \div 2 = 5$$
$$\begin{array}{r} 50 \\ 2\overline{)100} \end{array}$$

5. We do _____ problems.

   division   multiplication   problems

$$444 \ominus 123 = 321 \qquad \rule{2em}{0.8em}$$
$$\begin{array}{r} 77 \\ \ominus 16 \\ \hline 61 \end{array}$$

6. This is a _____ sign.

   lesser than   minus   plus

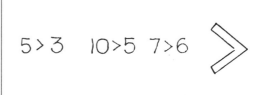

$$22 \times 2 \oslash 44$$
$$5 \times 5 \oslash 25$$
$$5 \cdot 5 \oslash 25 \qquad =$$

7. What's this sign?

   It's an _____ sign.

$$341 \oplus 802 = 1,143 \qquad +$$

8. This is a _____ sign.

   minus   plus   greater than

$$5 > 3 \quad 10 > 5 \quad 7 > 6 \qquad >$$

9. What's this sign?

   It's a _____ sign.

$$1 + 3 = \textcircled{4}$$

10. This is a _____ .

    percent   fraction   total

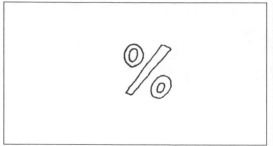

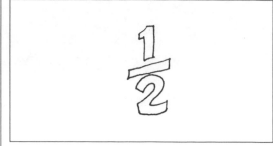

11. What's this?

     It's a _____ .

12. This is a _____ .

     fraction   decimal   percent sign

13. There are 13 girls and 12 boys in the Math class. How many students are there in the class?

14. My mother and father have seven children. How many people are there in my family?

15. There are twenty-five teachers in our school. Fifteen teachers are women. How many men teachers are there?

16. There are eight rooms in our house. We have four bedrooms. How many other rooms are there?

17. Every English student has two books. There are twelve students. How many books are there?

18. Every class has twenty-five students. There are five classes. How many students are there?

19. There are eighteen books in the room. Every student has three books. How many students are there?

20. Nelly rides the bus thirty blocks to school. The bus stops every three blocks. How many stops are there?

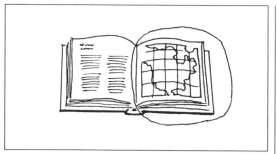

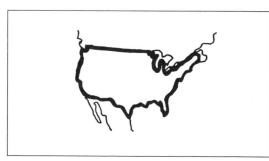

Social Studies Learning
(20 points)

1. This is a _____ .

    world   book   country

2. What's a country?

    It's a _____ .

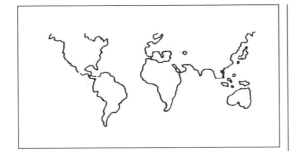

3. This is a map of the _____ .

   country   world   nation

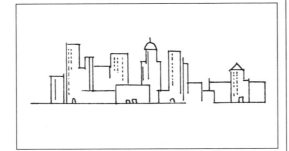

4. This is a _____ .

   river   city   people

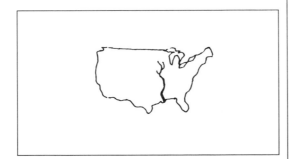

5. What's this?

   It's a _____ .

   people   city   river

6. In a city there are many _____ .

7. What's this?

   It's an _____ .

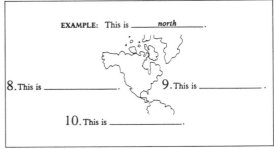

EXAMPLE: This is _____*north*_____ .

8. This is _____ .

9. This is _____ .

10. This is _____ .

EXAMPLE: This is _____*north*_____ .

8. This is _____ .

9. This is _____ .

10. This is _____ .

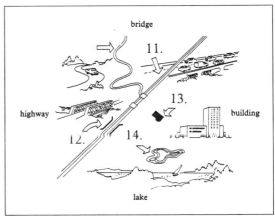

EXAMPLE: _____*road*_____

11. _____

12. _____

13. _____

14. _____

DIRECTIONS: Draw a line from the word for that region of the country to the states in that part of the country.

15. Southwestern   Delaware, Maryland, North Carolina, South Carolina, Virginia, West Virginia

16. Western   Connecticut, Maine, Massachusetts, New Hampshire, New Jersey, New York, Pennsylvania, Rhode Island, Vermont

17. Northeastern   Alabama, Arkansas, Florida, Georgia, Kentucky, Louisiana, Mississippi, Tennessee

18. Midwestern   California, Idaho, Montana, Oregon, Washington, Wyoming

19. Mid-Atlantic   Arizona, Colorado, Nevada, Oklahoma, Texas, Utah

20. Southern   Illinois, Indiana, Iowa, Kansas, Michigan, Minnesota, Missouri, Nebraska, North Dakota, South Dakota

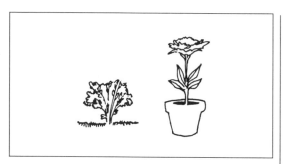 

Science Learning
(20 points)

1. We study _____ .

    plants   animals   trees

3. We learn about _____ .

    fish   birds   animals

2. What do you study?

    We study _____ .

4. What do you study?

    We study _____ .

5. We learn about _____ .

animals   birds   fish

6. We use a _____ .

microscope   moon   telescope

7. What's this?

It's the _____ .

8. We use a _____ .

telescope   star   microscope

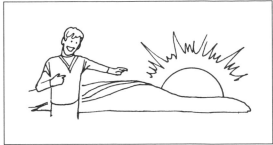

9. What's this?

It's the _____ .

10. We study the _____ .

stars   moon   microscope

11. What's this?

It's a _____ .

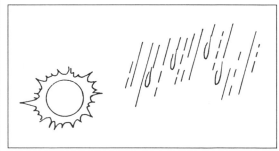

12. There are different _____ .

flowers   rains   seasons

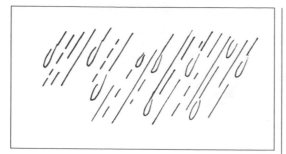

13. What's this?

It's _____ .

14. Every season has different _____ .

season   weather   rain

15. What do flowers do?

They _____ .

16. It is _____ .

hot   cold   up

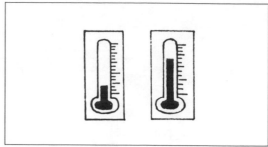

17. What do we learn from these?

We learn the _____ .

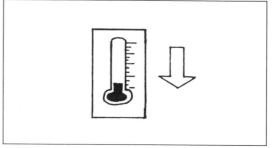

18. The temperature is going _____ .

up   hot   down

19. Is the weather hot or cold?

It's _____ .

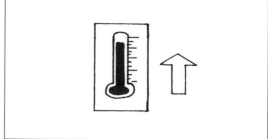

20. The temperature is going _____ .

up   cold   down

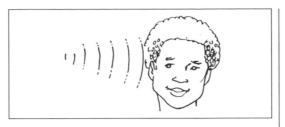

English Learning
(20 points)

1. What do you do?

   We _____ to English.

   talk   listen   words

5. What do you do in class?

   We _____ English.

   language   listen   speak

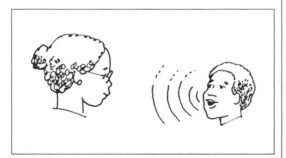

2. These are English _____ .

   listen   speak   words

6. We _____ English.

   write   read   paragraph

3. In class we _____ to the teacher.

   talk   listen   language

7. We _____ English.

   write   read   sentence

4. We are studying the English _____ .

   speak   language   listen

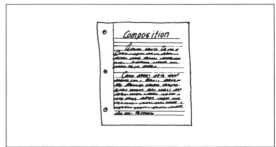

8. This is a _____ .

   composition   read   sentence

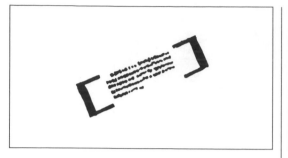

9. This is a _____ .

   write   paragraph   sentence

10. This is a _____ .

    composition   write   sentence

11. What are these?

    They're _____ .

12. This is a _____ .

    comma   period   question mark

13. What's this?

    It's a _____ a.

14. This is a _____ a.

    captial   small   comma

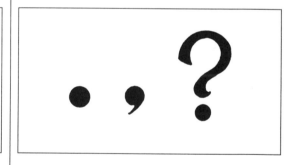

15. This is _____ .

    period   capital   punctuation

16. This is a _____ .

    date   letter   signature

17. This is a _____ .

comma   date   signature

18. This is a _____ .

date   comma   signature

19. This is a _____ .

question mark   period   comma

20. This is a _____ .

question mark   period   comma

Classroom and Minor Subject Learning
(20 points)

1. _____ a) Please be quiet.
   _____ b) Answer the question
   _____ c) Raise your hand.

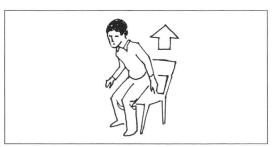

2. _____ a) Stand up.
   _____ b) Sit down.
   _____ c) Please be quiet.

3. _____ a) Copy the work.
   _____ b) Answer the question
   _____ c) Please be quiet.

4. _____ a) Close your book.
   _____ b) Take out your book.
   _____ c) Open your book.

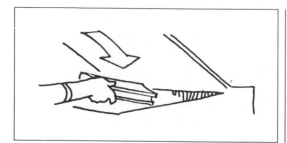

5. _____ a) Close your book.
   _____ b) Put away your book.
   _____ c) Take out your book.

6. They study _____ .

English   Science   Math

7. They study _____ .

Science   Social Studies   Math

8. They study _____ .

Social Studies   English   Science

9. They study _____ .

Math   Science   English

10. They take _____ .

Music   Art   Gym

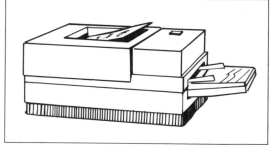

11. The printer is part of the computer

_____ .   screen   software   hardware

12. The computer talks to me on the

_____ .   printer   keyboard   screen

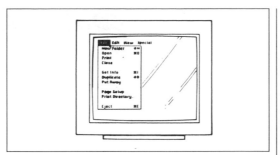

13. There is a _____ on the disk.

    boot   screen   program

17. These are _____ .

    colors   draw   picture

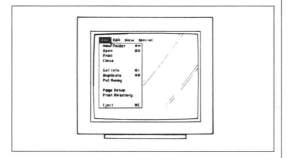

14. A program is _____ .

    screen   drive   software

18. We listen to the _____ .

    piano   tape   sing

15. I talk to the computer on the _____ .

    hardware   keyboard   printer

19. We listen to _____ .

    pianos   tapes   plays

16. In Art we _____ pictures

    crayon   color   paint

20. We _____ .

    play   song   sing

BOOK 2	TEST OF LESSONS 1–7

I. Alphabetical Order
(20 points)

Put the words in alphabetical order.

1. nice, good _____

2. baby, apple _____

3. six, twenty _____

4. more, love _____

5. time, up _____

6. Social Studies, English, Math _____

7. Art, Music, Gym _____

8. subtract, multiply, divide _____

9. correct, right, wrong _____

10. sun, moon, telescope _____

11. like, late _____

12. sew, star _____

13. cook, clean _____

14. sing, song _____

15. piano, play _____

16. stand, stop _____

17. boy, both _____

18. world, won't _____

19. thing, think _____

20. fine, find _____

II. The Library and Reference Books
(20 points)

A. THE LIBRARY

Finish the sentence with the correct word or words.

1. To find a book in the library you look in the _____ .

dictionary   reference   card catalog

2. The person who writes a book is the _____ .

   title   biography   author

3. The name of a book is the _____

   author   title   reference

4. In the dictionary words are in _____ .

   alphabetical order   card catalog   reference

5. A book that is true is _____ .

   biography   fiction   nonfiction

6. A book about someone is a _____ .

   biography   fiction   nonfiction

7. A book that tells us about people, places and things is an _____ .

   dictionary   fiction   encyclopedia

8. A book that tells stories is _____ .

   reference   nonfiction   fiction

9. A book that tells us about words is a _____ .

   reference   encyclopedia   dictionary

10. The dictionary and the encyclopedia are examples of _____ books.

   reference   fiction   biography

B. THE DICTIONARY

space   distance or area between or within
   things
Span'· ish   of or belonging to Spain
spare   extra scanty, not abundant
spark   a small, glowing piece of matter,
   especially from a fire

fāte, fär, fàst, fạll, finăl, cāre, at

Answer each question.

1. What word has an *A* pronounced like *care?* _____

2. What is the definition of *Spanish?* _____

3. What word has an *A* pronounced like *fate?* _____

4. What word has something to do with *fire?* _____

5. What is the definition of *space?* _____

C. THE ENCYCLOPEDIA

Write the answer.

Where do you look for information on

1. night   Volume _____   4. music   Volume _____

2. business   Volume _____   5. art   Volume _____

3. space   Volume _____

III. Parts of Books
(20 points)

A. THE TABLE OF CONTENTS

Answer each question.

1. On what page does the chapter about the new United States begin? _____

2. In what chapter can you read about John Jacob Astor, the Dutch fur trader? _____

3. What chapter tells about the American Indians who lived here before the Spanish came? _____

4. What chapter should you read to learn about the American Revolution? _____

5. What are the two chapters that tell about America's early settlers? _____

6. What chapter tells us about life in the colonies? _____

7. What chapter will tell about George Washington leading the American army? _____

8. What chapter will tell about Ponce de Leon, the Spanish explorer? _____

9. What chapter will tell about the English settling Virginia? _____

10. What chapter will tell about the first American president? _____

B. THE INDEX

Subjects, school, 5,7
  Vocabulary for
    Art, 29
    Computer, 27
    English, 21, 23, 45, 47
    Math, 13, 15, 37, 39
    Music, 31
    Science, 17, 19, 41, 43
    Shop, 25
    Social Studies, 9, 11, 33, 35, 49, 51
  Word problems in Math, 53–60

1. What pages have information on school subjects? _____

2. List 6 pages with information on Math. _____

3. How many pages have Social Studies vocabulary? _____

4. What page has the information on the word song? _____

5. Where do you find information on the word paint? _____

6. What page gives information on computer vocabulary? _____

7. What pages have information on English vocabulary? _____

8. How many pages have information on Science vocabulary? _____

9. Where do you find information on the word hardware? _____

10. How many pages give help on Math word problems? _____

IV. Life Reference Books
(20 points)

A. THE NEWSPAPER INDEX

Answer each question.

Where would you find

Around the Nation	6
Books	16
Business	31–41
Crossword	16
Editorials	24
Movies	12–16
Sports	19–23
TV/Radio	51
Weather	23

1. what movies are at the theaters? _____

2. when the news is on television tonight? _____

3. what the editor's opinions are? _____

4. the latest football scores? _____

5. the name of a good book to read? _____

A. THE TELEPHONE DIRECTORY

Finish each sentence.

1. You will find a friend's telephone number in the
   a) white pages   b) yellow pages   c) long distance

2. When you don't know a telephone number, you call
   a) emergency   b) long distance   c) information

3. When you need police officers, you call
   a) long distance   b) emergency   c) white pages

4. When you call another city, you are using
   a) yellow pages   b) long distance   c) white pages

5. When you want to find where to buy something, you look in the
   a) yellow pages   b) information   c) white pages

IV. Schedules and Diagrams
(20 points)

A. SCHEDULES
(10 points)

Use this train schedule to help answer the questions.

METROPOLITAN TRAINS			
TRAIN #	**TO:**	**DEPARTURE:**	**PLATFORM:**
5	Hastings	5:15	2
5A	Baytown	5:30	3
86	San Antonio	6:00	5
10	El Paso	6:15	2

1. I'm going to El Paso. When do I leave? _____

2. Mr. Niles wants to go to Baytown. What platform does he use? _____

3. The 6:00 train is leaving. Where does it go? _____

4. What number train do I take to Hastings? _____

5. What are the two trains that leave from the same platform? _____

B. DIAGRAMS
(10 points)

Use the organizational chart to answer the questions.

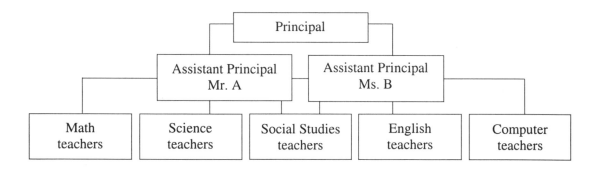

1. Who is the boss of the Assistant Principals? _____

2. Who is the boss of the Social Studies teachers? _____

3. Who is the boss of the Math teachers? _____

4. Who do the Science teachers work for? _____

5. Who do the Computer teachers work for? _____

BOOK 2   **TEST OF LESSONS 8–15**

I. Test Taking
(15 points)

A.

Read the sentence. Decide which answer is best. Write the letter of the correct answer on the line.

1. On some tests you must choose the correct answer from two or three possible

    a) answers   b) questions   c) corrects   _____

2. On some tests, you fill in

    a) an answer sheet   b) questions on the line   c) tests on the line   _____

3. On some tests, you write

    a) questions on the line   b) letters on the line   c) tests on the line   _____

4. On some tests, you write

    a) tests on the line   b) numbers on the line   c) questions on the line   _____

5. On some tests, you draw lines to

    a) make pictures   b) match columns   c) write tests   _____

B.

Complete the sentences. Write in the missing words.

Some tests have _____ with a _____ word or words. Sometimes the missing
                1   **2**

_____ are listed, and you must _____ them in. This is that kind of _____ .
  3   **4**   **5**

write   missing   test   words   sentences

A.

Complete the answer sheets with the information.

John Miller of Class 801. Birthday is September 1, 1976.

NAME			CLASS	DATE OF BIRTH
LAST	FIRST			MO. DAY YR

II. Writing Reports
(20 points)

A. REPORT FORM
(10 points)

1. John Miller is going to write a composition for Science. His Science teacher's name is Ms. Gordon. The date is February 4, 1992. The composition has the title "The Peaceful Use of Atomic Power."

Prepare the information in a correct composition form:

_____

_____

_____

_____

_____

2. Evelyn Diaz is going to write a report on a book she read by Sandra Cole. The book is *A House of Our Own,* and Evelyn liked it very much. The book tells the story of the Cole family, who move from house to house. They never have a house of their own. Then one day Mr. Cole saves enough money to buy one. Evelyn liked the book because she hopes that her family will have their own house some day.

Use this information to write Evelyn's book report.

(To Teacher: Any book report written on this information is acceptable. Grade on form and inclusion of the title, the author, the story and whether it was liked and why.)

B. LOCATING INFORMATION FOR A REPORT
(10 points)

Put the letter of the subject on the line next to each report title. You may use a subject more than one time.

a. Science   _____   1. "Famous Musicians"

b. Social Studies   _____   2. "Birds in the Southern United States"

c. Math   _____   3. "The History of Algebra"

d. Music   _____   4. "Early California Forts"

e. Art   _____   5. "Fun with Computers"

f. Computer   _____   6. "How to Enjoy Paintings"

     _____   7. "The First Computers"

     _____   8. "Egyptian Civilization—1000 B.C."

     _____   9. "Math in Your Daily Life"

     _____   10. "The Geography of Australia"

III. The Outline
(20 points)

A. (10 pts)

Here is an outline. It is not in correct order. Write it in correct order on the lines at the right.

1. Where she went to school   1. _____

2. Where she was born   2. _____

3. What she did later   3. _____

4. When she died   4. _____

5. Why we remember her   5. _____

B. (10 pts)

1. Tanya must write a composition for Art on the famous painter Pablo Picasso. In the library she found out that he was from Spain but lived in France most of his life. She found out that his most famous painting was *Guernica.* She also discovered that in his later life he did many things besides painting pictures. Write Tanya's outline for her here:

1. _____

2. _____

3. _____

4. _____

2. You must write a composition on how to do something. Choose something that you know well (riding a bicycle, cooking dinner, washing a car). Make an outline for your composition:

HOW TO _____

1.

2.

3.

4.

IV. The Summary
(20 points)

A. (10 points)   Choose the best summary for each paragraph.

1. My best friend is my brother Terry. He is two years older than I am, but that doesn't make any difference. We like to play the same games and eat the same food, and we even have the same friends. My mother says, "You and your brother are so much alike. You're almost twins."

SUMMARY A: My brother and I play the same games.
SUMMARY B: My mother says that we are twins.
SUMMARY C: My brother and I like the same things.

BEST SUMMARY: _____

2. It is not correct to say that the Spanish or the French or the English were the first Americans. People lived in America many thousands of years before the Europeans arrived. When Columbus came he thought these people were living in India, and he called them Indians.

SUMMARY A: Columbus called these people Indians.
SUMMARY B: The Spanish, French and English were the first Americans.
SUMMARY C: The first Americans were called Indians incorrectly.

BEST SUMMARY: _____

B (10 points) Find the short sentence in Column B that matches the long sentence in Column A. Write its number on the line.

COLUMN A

1. The birds were singing, there were beautiful flowers, and altogether it was a lovely day in May.

2. He gave us 15 pages of homework on Tuesday and 20 pages on Wednesday.

3. My cat jumps in bed every morning before I wake up to tell me that he's hungry and wants to eat.

4. We watch the news at 6, a space program at 7, and a movie from 8 till 10 every Tuesday night.

5. She is a good teacher because she always answers our questions and tries to be sure that we all understand.

COLUMN B

A. He wakes me up. _____

B. She helps us. _____

C. It was spring. _____

D. We had a lot of work. _____

E. We watch television from 6 to 10 on Tuesdays. _____

V. Judging Important Information
(20 points)

A (10 pts) Read the questions, then read the paragraph. Answer the questions after the paragraph.

1. Is it daytime or nighttime?

2. How many people are looking at the sky?

3. What season of the year is it?

4. Are the people inside or outdoors?

We sat and looked at the moon. The leaves of the trees around us moved gently in the summer breeze. The moon was as round and gold as the sun. He said to me, "I think about you all day. I dream about you every night." I listened to him and thought, he loves me.

1. You can find the answer to the first question in the

   a) last sentence   b) first sentence   c) second sentence   _____

2. You can find the answer to the second question in

   a) sentences 1 and 2   b) sentences 2 and 3   c) sentences 4 and 5   _____

3. You can find the answer to the third question in the

   a) first sentence   b) last sentence   c) second sentence   _____

4. You can find the answer to the fourth question in the

   a) first sentence   b) second sentence   c) last sentence   _____

5. The important sentences in this paragraph are

   a) first and last   b) first and second   c) only the last   _____

B. (10 points)   Read the questions, then read the paragraph. Draw a line through the sentences that are not important in the paragraph.

1.   What is a word for a rain and wind storm?

2.   How did the writer feel about the storm?

  It was frightening. The sky became as black as night. The wind grew stronger and stronger. My mother said, "Bring the dog and the cat inside. This is going to be bad." Soon the rain came. It was the first hurricane of the year.

BOOK 3	TEST OF LESSONS 1–8

I. Dictionary Skills
(30 points)

A. UNDERSTANDING DEFINITIONS
(16 pts)

Write the number or letter of the correct definition for *present* on the line next to each sentence.

present *adj.* 1. being at hand in a given place 2. existing at this time; not past or future; 3. instant or immediate *n.* a gift or donation *v.* 1. to introduce 2. to bring to view; display 3. to offer as a gift

1.   How many students are present in the classroom? _____

2.   We presented him with a book. _____

3.   What shall we buy for a present? _____

4.   Sherry is the present secretary of our club. _____

5.   The theater presented one of Shakespeare's plays. _____

6.   My aunt was presented to the mayor of Houston. _____

7.   I gave her a Mother's Day present. _____

8.   There are no jobs at the present time. _____

B. PRONUNCIATION
(14 pts)

Find an example word from the pronunciation key for each word below. Copy it on the line beside the dictionary pronunciation.

1.   luck (lək) _____

2.   dip (dip) _____

3.   moth (môth) _____

4.   team (tēm) _____

5.   show (shō) _____

6.   take (tāk) _____

7.   tool (tül) _____

a	bat, sat	oi	boy, oil
ā	ate, late	ou	how, out
ä	jar, far	ə	cup, about
e	met, get	u̇	put, look
ē	equal, easy	ü	rule, food
ėr	term, bird		
i	sit, is		
ī	ice, my		
o	top, stop		
ō	open, coat		
ô	order, more		

II. Categorizing
   (20 points)

A. (10 pts)   Put the words in one of the three categories.

		PEOPLE	COLORS	PLACES
man	white	_____	_____	_____
blue	girl	_____	_____	_____
red	apartment	_____	_____	_____
school	building	_____	_____	_____
teacher	yellow	_____	_____	_____

Write the missing word on the line.

1. April, November, May   are examples of _____

2. bus, train, automobile   are examples of _____

3. nineteen, second, three   are examples of _____

4. eggs, bread, fish   are examples of _____

5. fire, accident, death   are examples of _____

6. football, baseball, tennis   are examples of _____

7. tomorrow, today, yesterday   are examples of _____

8. secretary, executive, foreman are examples of _____

9. movie, restaurant, television are examples of _____

10. song, record, dance   are examples of _____

MISSING WORDS:

food   months   emergencies   music   jobs   numbers   time   sports   transportation   entertainments

III. Analogies
   (40 points)

A.   **SYNONYMS**
     (10 pts)

Complete the analogy. Write the letter of the correct synonym on the line.

1. right : correct :: wrong : a) correct b) false c) good   _____

2. like : love :: test : a) exam b) teacher c) class   _____

3. painting : picture :: home : a) school b) house c) family   _____

4. read : study :: lamp : a) house b) room c) light   _____

5. large : big :: good : a) delicious b) nasty c) easy   _____

B.   ANTONYMS
(10 pts)

Complete the analogy. Write the letter of the correct antonyms on the line.

1.   often : never : : correct : a) good b) right c) wrong   _____

2.   old : young : : pretty : a) nice b) ugly c) lovely   _____

3.   up : down : : little : a) big b) small c) good   _____

4.   dirty : clean : : happy : a) pleased b) sad c) glad   _____

5.   antonym : synonym : : breakfast : a) meal b) dinner c) food   _____

C.   NUMBERS
(10 pts)

Write the letter of the correct number to complete the number analogy on the line.

1.   11 : 0 : : 12 : a) 2 b) 0 c) 3   _____

2.   9 : 64 : : 7 : a) 49 b) 35 c) 63   _____

3.   3 : 6 : : 8 : a) 16 b) 10 c) 4   _____

4.   20 : 4 : : 25 : a) 9 b) 10 c) 5   _____

5.   8 : 15 : : 20 : a) 25 b) 27 c) 30   _____

D.   PART TO WHOLE
(10 pts)

Complete the analogy. Write the correct letter on the line.

1.   foot : man : : teacher : a) school b) student c) room   _____

2.   October : year : : bed : a) sleep b) bathroom c) bedroom   _____

3.   eye : face : : son : a) father b) family c) mother   _____

4.   food : meal : : word : a) language b) see c) class   _____

5.   brake : car : : light : a) sun b) dark c) window   _____

IV. Synthesizing and Concluding
(10 points)

Write the letter of the correct meaning on the line.

1.   There were so many people at the party that we couldn't sit down

   MEANS   a) There were no chairs.   _____

         b) People stood on the chairs.   _____

         c) There was not much room.   _____

2.   The movie frightened me, but it was interesting

   MEANS   a) I didn't like the movie.   _____

         b) I didn't see the movie.   _____

         c) I liked the movie.   _____

3.   She may be intelligent, but she's not very nice

   MEANS   a) I like her.   _____

         b) I don't like her.   _____

         c) I don't know her.   _____

4. We ran out of the burning building

    MEANS   a) We had a fire at our house.   ——————

                   b) There was a fire.   ——————

                   c) There were two of us.   ——————

5. Always pay attention to the teacher in class

    MEANS   a) Don't do your homework.   ——————

                   b) Don't go to class.   ——————

                   c) Don't stop listening.   ——————

V. Predicting
(20 points)

A. NEXT SENTENCE
(10 pts)

Read each group of sentences. Decide which sentence will be next and write an *X* next to it.

1. When our class needed money for a trip, we talked with our teacher. "There are many things we can do," she said, "but we all must help with the work."

    —————— a) We said that we'd all help.

    —————— b) We said that we wouldn't help.

    —————— c) We said that she'd help.

2. The friends were walking home after school. Don said to Leroy, "Do you understand the homework? I don't know how to do it." Leroy answered, "Sure, I understand it.

    —————— a) It's too bad that you don't."

    —————— b) You must be stupid."

    —————— c) Come inside with me and I'll help you."

3. Every Saturday morning, Mrs. Way tells her son, "I want you to clean up your room. Don't say that you have to go out. First, you must take care of your room." And every Saturday her son answers,

    —————— a) "I'll be glad to clean it up."

    —————— b) Oh, Ma. I have to go out this morning."

    —————— c) "I'm tired."

4. There are nice people everywhere. Yesterday I was downtown. I had to meet my friend at Fourth and Main, but I didn't know where that was. A nice lady that I asked for help

    —————— a) walked me right to the corner of Fourth and Main.

    —————— b) said, "Get lost, sonny."

    —————— c) said, "I don't know where it is."

5. My cousin Kim is coming to visit us next week. I don't know him, but my aunt is very nice. I think that probably he'll

    —————— a) be nice, too.

    —————— b) not be nice, too.

    —————— c) speak English.

B. PREDICTING THE END OF WRITING
(10 pts)

Read each paragraph. Decide which prediction is true and write an X on the line next to it.

1. Everyone in our family is working. My mother takes care of children at home. My father works in a factory. My brother and I work every Saturday at the supermarket.

_____ a) Next the writer will talk about the supermarket.

_____ b) Next the writer will talk about his brother.

_____ c) Next the writer will talk about what his family does with their money.

2. October can be a beautiful month in the Northeastern United States. The weather is usually cool and sunny. The leaves of the trees become red and gold.

_____ a) Next the writer will tell more about October.

_____ b) Next the writer will tell more about winter.

_____ c) Next the writer will tell more about trees.

3. Those were difficult years for the young United States. No one knew whether democracy would really work. There were countries in Europe that owned part of the land on the continent. Some of this ended with the Louisiana Purchase.

_____ a) Next the writer will tell about democracy.

_____ b) Next the writer will tell about the Louisiana Purchase.

_____ c) Next the writer will tell about Europe.

4. My friend has a pet rabbit named Coney. Coney is very funny. He likes to play games with my friend. Sometimes he gets behind a chair and hops out very suddenly.

_____ a) Next the writer will tell of other things that Coney does.

_____ b) Next the writer will tell about his dog.

_____ c) Next the writer will tell about his friend.

5. "Take my hand," said the fire fighter. "Don't be afraid." I looked down at the street. We were so high that the cars were very small. My mother pushed me. "Go," she said, "but be careful."

_____ a) Next the writer will tell about escaping from a fire.

_____ b) Next the writer will tell why there was a fire.

_____ c) Next the writer will tell about the fire fighter.

BOOK 3	TEST OF LESSONS 9–15

I. Facts and Opinions
(20 points)

Decide which sentences are facts and which are opinions. Write F on the line next to the fact sentences. Write O on the line next to the opinion sentences.

1. That's a very ugly building over there. _____

2. We were late getting to school this morning. _____

3. I like your blue dress. _____

4. My country is quite small. _____

5. "All my friends are nice," she said. _____

6. All my friends are nice. _____

7. Mr. Fine opened the window and called to George. _____

8. The movie tickets were five dollars each. _____

9. The movie was terrible. _____

10. Love and hate are emotions. _____

II. Cause and Effect
(20 pts)

These sentences are not complete. Some are missing CAUSE (C). Some are missing EFFECT (E). Write C or E for the part that is missing.

1. Because we were early. _____

2. The bus stopped at the corner. _____

3. Everyone shouted. _____

4. Because she likes ice cream. _____

5. And we all went to sleep. _____

6. So Mrs. Miller gave me the book. _____

7. I got 100 on the test. _____

8. Because they ran upstairs. _____

9. Because she smiled. _____

10. We all had a good time. _____

III. Hidden Meaning
(20 pts)

Decide which meaning is correct for these paragraphs. Write an X next to your choice.

1. "That's nice," said her mother. "I work all day in that hot factory. Then I come home and start cooking for your father. Then I wash your clothes and iron them. I love it when you don't take care of them."

The writer wants us to understand that

_____ a) Her mother likes to work at the factory.

_____ b) Her mother wants the girl to take care of her clothes.

_____ c) Her mother doesn't want the girl to take care of her clothes.

2. "Oh, I'm sorry," said Jeannine. Her friend answered, "That's all right. I really didn't want to go out with him. I don't really like rich, good-looking men."

The friend really

_____ a) did want to go out with him.

_____ b) didn't want to go out with him.

_____ c) didn't know him.

3. The lady at the library said, "No, go ahead and talk. It's very interesting to hear all about your new clothes. I'm sure that everyone who is reading wants to know about them, too."

The writer wants us to understand that

_____ a) It's interesting to hear about clothes.

_____ b) You should talk at the library.

_____ c) You should be quiet at the library.

4. Life can be beautiful. Remember that when your best friend is nasty to you. Remember that when you fall downstairs and break your leg. Remember that when you don't pass your Science test.

The writer is really saying that

_____ a) Life can be beautiful.

_____ b) Sometimes life isn't beautiful.

_____ c) Your best friend is beautiful.

IV. Mood, Figurative Meaning
(20 points)

A. MOOD
(10 pts)

Read the paragraphs and then the questions. Choose the correct answer and write the letter on the line.

"You're going to get married?" said my mother. "Oh, dear." My father smiled. "Well, it"s about time," he said. I looked at my mother. What was wrong with her? Why couldn't she like Jim?

1. The father is   a) ashamed   b) happy   c) sad   _____

2. The mother is   a) proud   b) angry   c) sad   _____

3. I am   a) ashamed   b) angry   c) sad   _____

"Who do you think you are?" she shouted at me. "You think you're special because you get good grades? Well, you're not. So there." I began to cry.

1. She is   a) ashamed   b) angry   c) proud

2. I am   a) angry   b) happy   c) sad

B. FIGURATIVE MEANING
(10 pts)

Many special meanings are comparisons. Read the phrases below and then select the best word to complete them.

1. That cat is so fat that she's as big as

   a) a house   b) a cat   c) a chair   _____

2. When he gets angry he gets as red as

   a) a tomato   b) red   c) my hand   _____

3. Sometimes you seem as far away as

   a) downtown   b) next door   c) the moon   _____

4. The storm made the sky as black as

   a) a cloud   b) night   c) rain   _____

5. He said, "I love you more than

   a) my dog."   b) my brother."   c) my life."   _____

Teacher's Guide: Word Lists, Activities, and Answers

Lesson 1	Classroom Directions, Page 1

VOCABULARY

Answer the question.	Please be quiet.	Sit down.
Close your book.	Put away your book.	Stand up.
Copy the work.	Raise your hand.	Take out your book.
Open your book.	Read.	Write.

REINFORCEMENT ACTIVITIES

In Content Classroom:

1. Give student(s) aural-oral practice on whole-class or one-to-one basis through games: Simon Says, charades, drawing task slips.

2. Add or expand directions with classroom vocabulary that can be demonstrated. (*open/close* the *door/window,* substitution of *notebook* for book).

In ESL Classroom:

1. Expansion drill with *please*. Substitution drill with *work/book.*

2. Teach and drill conversion of simple command to first person present, *Close the book* to *I close the book.*

3. Teach and drill conversion of first person to second person present, *I answer the question* to *You answer the question.*

Answers

Page 2	Page 4
1. C	1. B
2. B	2. C
3. A	3. B
4. B	4. A
5. A	5. C
6. C	6. A

Lesson 2	Classroom Subjects, Page 5

VOCABULARY

| Art | English | Math (Mathematics) | Science |
| Computer | Gym | Music | Social Studies |

**REINFORCEMENT
ACTIVITIES**

In Content Classroom:

1. Require student(s) to have clearly labeled sections of a notebook or separate notebooks for each subject. Present oral reinforcement using vocabulary from Lesson 1: *Open your Social Studies book. Take out your Science book.*

2. Give student(s) large ruled chart of school days and school periods. Have student(s) complete the chart according to an actual schedule.

In ESL Classroom:

1. Drill conversion of *you/I* with previous and new vocabulary.

2. Practice responses *Yes, I do, No, I don't* to *Do you . . . ?* questions.

3. Drill conversion of *study/have/take* with subject names.

Answers

Page 6, Page 8   This will vary according to individual schedules.

Lesson 3	Social Studies, Page 9

VOCABULARY

| book | country | map | ocean | river |
| city | land | nation | people | world |

**REINFORCEMENT
ACTIVITES**

In Content Classroom

1. Use the student(s) Social Studies materials to check aural-oral comprehension. Ask the question *What's this?* and require the answer *It's . . .*

2. Check the Social Studies vocabulary list at the back of this manual. Then add to the above list any words not taught in this book but appropriate to your course. Show the student pictures or real things that illustrate each word. Practice correct pronunciation, and require that the student's notebook have a permanent list of these additions.

In ESL Classroom:

1. Practice *What's this?* questions with variant responses: *This is/It's.*

2. Conversion drill: *This is/These are.*

3. Conversion drill: *There is/There are.*

Answers

Page 10

1. book
2. map
3. world
4. nation
5. book
6. country
7. world
8. nation

Page 12

1. people
2. city
3. ocean
4. river
5. city
6. people
7. ocean
8. river

Lesson 4	Math (Mathematics), Page 13

VOCABULARY

add	divide	multiplication	number	subtract
addition	division	multiply	problem	subtraction

REINFORCEMENT ACTIVITIES

In Content Classroom:

1. Practice aural comprehension with student(s) by writing two numbers on chalkboard for whole-class or on large paper for individuals or small groups. Say "Copy the numbers," then, going slowly, have students do all four functions with the numbers, showing you results each time. Reinforce with questions such as, "What's this?" modeling the reply "It's addition/subtraction/multiplication/division."

2. Check the Math (Mathematics) vocabulary list at the back of this manual. Then add to the above list any words not taught in this book but necessary to your course at the present time. Demonstrate the meaning of the vocabulary through actual problems. Practice correct pronunciation and require that the student's notebook have a permanent list of these additions.

In ESL Classroom:

1. Conversion of *We* + math verb/*It's a(n)* math adjective *problem.*

2. Question-answer drill with *What do we do?/We* + math verb.

3. Question-answer drill *What are these?/They're (They are).*

Answers

Page 14

1.	numbers	5.	multiply
2.	multiply	6.	subtract
3.	divide	7.	add
4.	add	8.	numbers

Page 16

1.	addition	5.	division
2.	subtraction	6.	problems
3.	problems	7.	subtraction
4.	division	8.	multiplication

Lesson 5	Science, Page 17

VOCABULARY

animal	fish	moon	star	telescope
bird	microscope	plant	sun	tree

REINFORCEMENT ACTIVITIES

In Content Classroom:

1. Practice aural-oral comprehension with student(s) by using Science charts and instruments. Use question *What do we learn about in Science?* as well as *What do we study?*

2. Check the Science vocabulary list at the back of this manual. Then add to the above list any words not taught in this book but useful in your course at the present time. Use real objects or pictures to demonstrate meaning. Practice correct pronunciation and require that the student's notebook have a permanent list of these vocabulary additions.

In ESL Classroom:

1. Drill conversion of all previous verbs from *I* to *We.*

2. Drill question-answer *What do you* (previous verb)?/*We* (verb).

3. Reinforce *What do you use?/What do you see?* with previous and present vocabulary nouns.

Answers

Page 18

1.	animals	5.	plants
2.	trees	6.	fish
3.	plants	7.	birds
4.	birds	8.	animals

Page 20

1.	microscope	5.	stars
2.	sun	6.	moon
3.	telescope	7.	microscope
4.	stars	8.	sun

Lesson 6	**English, Page 21**

VOCABULARY

composition	listen	read	speak	word
language	paragraph	sentence	talk	write

REINFORCEMENT ACTIVITIES

In Content Classroom:

1. Practice aural-oral comprehension of student(s) by using command forms for verbs taught. Particularly in a class of students from varied backgrounds, question students with *What language do you speak?*

2. Check the English vocabulary list at the back of this manual. Then add to the above list any words not taught in this book but necessary to your course at the present time. Demonstrate meaning. Practice correct pronunciation and require that the student's notebook have a permanent list of these vocabulary additions.

In ESL Classroom:

1. Conversion drill of question *What do you* (verb)? to *What are you doing? I'm . . .*

2. Conversion drill of *We* + simple present to *We* + present progressive.

3. Introduce *I* and *you* with present progressive of known verbs.

Answers

Page 22

1.	listen	5.	speak
2.	words	6.	words
3.	language	7.	listen
4.	talk	8.	speak

Page 24

1.	composition	5.	write
2.	read	6.	composition
3.	sentence	7.	paragraph
4.	write	8.	read

Lesson 7	**Computer, Page 25**

VOCABULARY

boot	disk drive	floppy disk	keyboard	program	screen
disk	display	hardware	printer	software	

REINFORCEMENT ACTIVITIES

In Content Classroom:

1. Practice aural-oral comprehension with student(s) by using the real objects in your classroom. Aside from the vocabulary nouns, practice verbs with questions like *What do we use?* Require complete answers.

2. Expand the computer vocabulary to include words useful to your own course. Demonstrate the meaning of the words. Practice correct pronunciation and require that the student's notebook have a permanent list of these vocabulary additions.

In ESL Classroom:

1. Conversion drill: *I* to *we* and *you* to *he/she*.

2. Conversion drill: simple present to present progressive with known verbs.

Answers

Page 26			Page 28		
1. display	5. keyboard		1. disk drive	5. disk	
2. hardware	6. printer		2. boot	6. program	
3. printer	7. screen		3. program	7. boot	
4. screen	8. display		4. software	8. disk drive	

Lesson 8	Art/Music, Page 29

VOCABULARY

color	draw	piano	play	song
crayon	paint	picture	sing	tape

REINFORCEMENT ACTIVITIES

In Content Classroom:

1. Practice aural-oral comprehension with student(s) by using the real objects in your classroom. Use the questions *What is this?* requiring the answer *It's . . .* and *What am I doing?* requiring the answer *You're . . .* The verb *making* may be substituted for *doing*.

2. According to the needs of your course, add vocabulary words useful to the student. Be sure the meaning of the words is clear through the use of pictures or real objects. Practice pronunciation and require students to maintain a permanent list of these words in a notebook.

In ESL Classroom:

1. Expansion drills with *sometimes* and with *many*.

2. Conversion drills of *we* to *he/she* using lesson verbs. Conversion drills of simple present to present progressive using lesson verbs.

3. Drill question-answer *What does* (noun) *do?* and (Noun) + verb + *s*.

Answers

Page 30			Page 32		
1. picture	5. paint		1. piano	5. plays	
2. draw	6. draw		2. sing	6. tapes	
3. crayons	7. colors		3. tapes	7. sing	
4. paint	8. pictures		4. plays	8. songs	

Lesson 9	Social Studies, Page 33

VOCABULARY	bridge	direction	highway	north	south
	building	east	lake	road	west

REINFORCEMENT ACTIVITES

In Content Classroom:

1. Reinforce understanding of the directions with map reading material from your course. In addition, have students draw maps of their local community, identifying the school and their home.

2. After consulting the Social Studies vocabulary list at the end of this manual, expand the student(s)' vocabulary with your own choice of words. You may, for instance, want to teach *up, down, left, right.*

In ESL Classroom:

1. Expansion drill with *some.*

2. Conversion drill: *some* to *many.*

3. Expansion drill with the tag *too.*

Answers

Page 34

1. west   east
         south

2. Check to see that directions have been followed exactly.

Lesson 10	Math, Page 37

VOCABULARY	decimal	fraction	less than	percent	total
	equal	greater than	minus	plus	whole

REINFORCEMENT ACTIVITIES

In Content Classroom:

1. Reinforce aural-oral understanding by placing appropriate problems on the chalkboard or a large piece of paper. Have students read the problems aloud. Reverse this procedure by using dictation.

2. After checking the Math vocabulary list at the back of this manual, add any new words which are appropriate for your course. You may, for example, want to teach some common fractions (1/2, 1/3, 1/4) emphasizing particularly the *-th* ending used to form most fractions.

In ESL Classroom:

1. Unless students are sufficiently advanced in English, practice the contrast of *more than/less than.*

2. Conversion drill *more than* to *greater than.*

3. If student(s) are sufficiently advanced, practice short *when* clauses with students terminating sentences, for example *When we work on computers, we use the keyboard.*

Answers

Page 38

1.	a less than	5.	an equal
2.	a minus	6.	a greater than
3.	a plus	7.	a minus
4.	a greater than	8.	a plus

Page 40

1.	total	5.	whole number
2.	percent sign	6.	decimal
3.	whole number	7.	percent sign
4.	fraction	8.	total

Lesson 11	**Science, Page 41**

VOCABULARY

cold	flower	hot	season	up
down	grow	rain	temperature	weather

REINFORCEMENT ACTIVITIES

In Content Classroom:

1. Reinforce aural-oral understanding of vocabulary by requiring students to give a brief daily weather report. In the beginning you may have to cue the information with such questions as *Is there sun? Is it raining?* and *What is the temperature?*

2. After checking the Science vocabulary list at the back of this manual, add more useful words to the student's permanent notebook list. You might expand by presenting additional vocabulary for the four seasons, such as *snow, fog, wet* and *dry.*

In ESL Classroom:

1. Conversion drill: *up/down* and *hot/cold.* Drill *Is it . . . or . . . ?* with answers.

2. Expansion drill with *different.*

3. Various drills with *When?* question-answers such as *When do you go to Social Studies?*

Answers

Page 42

1.	rain	5.	flower
2.	seasons	6.	grow
3.	flower	7.	rain
4.	weather	8.	season

Page 44

1.	hot	5.	going up
2.	down	6.	hot
3.	cold	7.	going down
4.	up	8.	temperature

Lesson 12	**English, Page 45**

VOCABULARY

capital	date	letter (written form)	punctuation	signature
comma	letter (of alphabet)	period	question mark	small

REINFORCEMENT ACTIVITIES

In Content Classroom:

1. Do an aural-oral review of material in both lessons. Punctuation is not standardized among all languages. Even so small a thing as a date may be written differently from culture to culture. Work with desk or chalkboard examples to be sure students understand what the specific meaning of the punctuation is.

2. Give student(s) various exercises to strengthen correct punctuation usage. In one the task may be to encircle all periods. In another the task could be to underline all capital letters. Have students make a "style book" to keep permanently in their notebooks.

In ESL Classroom:

1. Drill oral spelling with capital letters. First have students read and spell from words on chalkboard. Progress to a spelling bee.

2. Teach the written letter form with body, salutation, date, closing and signature. In shortening dates (8/12/93) be sure to check that students are placing the month first.

Answers

Page 46

1. My teacher is Ms. James. She is teaching me about punctuation. I know what a capital letter is. I know when to use it, too. I like English.

2. In English we are writing sentences. Sentences begin with a capital letter. Sentences end with a period. This is part of punctuation.

Page 48

1. date

2. question mark

3. signature

4. letter

5–8. Check to see that lines are drawn correctly.

Lesson 13	**Social Studies, Page 49**

VOCABULARY

N.B. The names of all states are covered in the reading material. They are not taught as separate vocabulary to be learned.

Mid-Atlantic	Northeastern	Southwestern	Western
Midwestern	Southern	states	

REINFORCEMENT ACTIVITIES

In Content Classroom:

1. If possible, the maps in the student book should be supplemented by larger ones from your own material. You may want students to use a reproduction of a United States map to color-code the various regions of the country.

2. You may want students to memorize and maintain a permanent list in a notebook of all the states and their regions.

In ESL Classroom:

1. Continue oral spelling work, using the names of the states.

2. Reinforce previous punctuation learning by giving a number of sentences in which state names need to be capitalized.

Answers

Pages 50, 52   Check to see that lines are drawn correctly.

Lesson 14	**Math, Page 53**

VOCABULARY

REINFORCEMENT
ACTIVITIES

In Content Classroom: Cardinal numbers: one–nineteen; twenty–one hundred by 10's; thousand and zero; million; billion and ordinals; first–tenth

In ESL Classroom:

1. Give student(s) simple addition and subtraction problems. Have student(s) convert numbers to their written counterparts.

2. Direct students to copy and maintain permanently in a notebook the written counterparts for all cardinal and ordinal numbers given here.

Answers

1. Reinforce aural-oral understanding of numbers with simple games such as Bingo or Seven-up.

2. Using real objects and pictures, present simple addition or subtraction problems with the question *How many . . . ?*

Page 54

1. 3 brothers + 4 sisters = 7 brothers and sisters

2. 3 boys + 4 girls = 7 friends

3. 10 pencils + 12 pencils = 22 pencils

4. 6 Western states + 11 Midwestern + 6 Southwestern states = 23 states in the West, Midwest and Southwest

Page 56

1. 6 subjects – 3 subjects before lunch = 3 subjects after lunch

2. 35 teachers – 6 are my teachers = 29 other teachers

3. 5 schoolbooks – 1 English book = 4 other books

Lesson 15	**Math, Page 57**

20 words – 10 words he knows now = 10 more he needs to learn

REINFORCEMENT
ACTIVITIES

In Content Classroom: **SKILL OBJECTIVE:** Learning to read Math multiplication and division word problems

1. Continue work with written numbers by having students convert simple multiplication and division problems to words.

2. Require students to memorize and recite multiplication tables. Some may need to retain

| In ESL Classroom: | 1. | Reinforce aural-oral use of numbers through games that require some multiplication or division such as Yahtzee© or Scrabble©. |
| | 2. | Require students to write their own simple multiplication and division word problems. Have students quiz one another. |

Answers

Page 58

1. 2 sandwiches × 30 students = 60 sandwiches

2. 2 letters × 8 students = 16 letters

3. 3 crayons × 12 students = 36 crayons

4. 5 rooms × 4 floors = 20 rooms

Page 60

1. 20 rooms ÷ 5 rooms on each floor = 4 floors

2. 18 students ÷ 6 machines = 3 students for each machine

3. 15 pages ÷ 3 days = 5 pages each day

4. 10 pieces of fish ÷ 5 people = 2 pieces of fish for each person

BOOK 2

| **Lesson 1** | **Alphabetical Order, Page 1** |

SKILL OBJECTIVE: Learning to alphabetize by letter and by two letters

REINFORCEMENT ACTIVITIES

In Content Classroom:	1.	Assign a group of letters to each student. Using the vocabulary list for your content area in the back of this manual give students a list of words and time them while they find the words that fall into their own letter categories. Do this several times, varying assigned letter groups and lists.
	2.	Introduce students to a simple number code (A = 1, Z = 26). Use code to write special messages or instructions.
In ESL Classroom:	1.	Consider using any of the suggestions for the Content Classroom. In addition, add your own alphabetizing exercises such as the ones on Page 4.
	2.	Practice aural-oral discrimination through dictation of words to be alphabetized. Follow through with lessons on such confusers as initial *s* and *th*.

Answers

Page 2

A.	**B.**
1. M, N, O	1. apple
2. S, T, U	2. bank
3. D, E, F	3. can
4. X, Y, Z	4. girl
5. J, K, L	5. job
6. P, Q, R	6. look
7. G, H, I	7. man
8. U, V, W	8. plant
9. B, C, D	9. reference
10. N, O, P	10. song
11. H, I, J	11. television
12. W, X, Y	12. ugly
13. E, F, G	13. woman
14. T, U, V	14. zebra

Page 4

A.	**B.**	**C.**
2. dark, dry	2. opaque, open	2. car, chance, cheer
3. right, round	3. nail, name	3. veil, very, vowel
4. sing, song	4. fan, fat	4. mess, moon, more
5. go, green	5. this, three	5. has, hat, have
6. like, love	6. had, have	6. slow, stop, student
7. part, play	7. look, love	7. bank, bill, book
8. nice, no	8. stand, student	8. eat, emergency, every
9. bank, book	9. fill, find	9. the, thing, too
10. emergency, excellent	10. they, think	10. dead, dear, do

Lesson 2	**The Library, Page 5**

SKILL OBJECTIVE: Learning about the library

VOCABULARY	alphabetical order	card	encyclopedia	reference
	author	catalog	fiction	subject
REINFORCEMENT ACTIVITIES	biography	dictionary	nonfiction	title

In Content Classroom:

1. Using classroom or library books, have students practice aural-oral reinforcement of vocabulary. Ask such questions as *What is the title? Is this a reference book?* or *Is this a dictionary or an encyclopedia?*

2. If possible, arrange for all students to visit the library. Ask the librarian to show students the real objects that illustrate vocabulary.

In ESL Classroom:

1. Follow any suggestion for the Content Classroom teacher. In addition, try to arrange a library card for student(s).

2. Using the materials on your own shelves, have student(s) make up library catalog cards for your books.

3. Ask student(s) to bring to class one example each of a biography, a fiction book, a nonfiction book and a reference book. If there is only limited access to books, have student make his or her own book and illustrate it.

Answers

Page 6

B.

3. K	8. M	13. A
4. A	9. S	14. R
5. R	10. L	15. B
6. W	11. D	
7. H	12. G	

Page 8

A.

1. nonfiction
2. dictionary
3. fiction
4. encyclopedia
5. biography

Lesson 3	**The Dictionary, The Encyclopedia, Page 9**

SKILL OBJECTIVE: Learning how to use reference books

REINFORCEMENT ACTIVITIES

In Content Classroom:

1. Give student(s) a list of words pertinent to your subject area. Require students to keep a permanent list of words and their definitions as given in a classroom or library dictionary.

2. Assign student(s) different topics to be researched in a classroom or library encyclopedia. Depending on maturity and English level of student(s), topics may be researched by noting just the pages on which information can be found in a specific encyclopedia or by copying actual information.

In ESL Classroom:

1. Require student(s) to use word lists in a native-language English dictionary of his/her/their own.

2. Using any encylopedia(s) available (desk to multi-volume), give student(s) several exercises similar to those on Page 12.

Answers

Page 10

A.

1. one side of a sheet of paper in a book
2. page
3. the inside of your hand between your fingers and your wrist *or* a tall tropical tree
4. the feeling of hurt

B.

1. a chief or leader
2. a very large rock or stone
3. liquid
4. on your arm

Page 12

A.

2. Volume 3
3. Volume 1
4. Volume 1
5. Volume 1
6. Volume 3
7. Volume 1
8. Volume 5
9. Volume 6
10. Volume 1

B.

2. Volume 1
3. Volume 1
4. Volume 2
5. Volume 1
6. Volume 1
7. Volume 5
8. Volume 3
9. Volume 6
10. Volume 3

Lesson 4	The Table of Contents, The Index, Page 13

SKILL OBJECTIVE: Learning how to locate information in a book

REINFORCEMENT ACTIVITIES

In Content Classroom:

1. Use your subject text to give aural-oral reinforcement to learning. Ask student(s) questions about the Table of Contents. If the book is indexed, use that for another lesson on finding information in books.

2. Give student(s) other texts with accompanying written questions on the Table of Contents and the Index.

In ESL Classroom:

1. Have student(s) examine all subject texts being used. Discuss with them the similarities and differences in the ways Tables of Contents and Indexes are organized.

2. Teach the basic Roman numerals which are often used in books and may be confusing to ESL students from countries where they are not used.

Answers

Page 14

1. Chapters 1, 2, 3, 4
2. Page 72
3. Chapter 6
4. Chapter 1
5. Chapter 4

Page 16

A.

1. Pages 17, 19, 41, 43
2. Page 30
3. Pages 5, 7
4. Pages 53-60 (also perhaps Pages 13, 15, 37, 39)
5. Page 31

B.

1. Page 640
2. Page 141
3. Pages 667, 672
4. Page 170

Lesson 5	Newspaper Index/The Telephone Directory, Page 17

SKILL OBJECTIVE: Learning how to locate information in everyday references

REINFORCEMENT ACTIVITIES

In Content Classroom:

1. Require student(s) to bring to class newspaper stories on topics pertinent to your subject area. Working in pairs or small groups, have students make one-page newspapers, using their clippings. Ask each group to develop an index for its newspaper.

2. Assign student(s) the task of gathering telephone numbers of useful places or organizations, such as Police, Fire, Housing. Have each make an alphabetical telephone directory of the numbers.

In ESL Classroom:

1. Write (or, according to level, have students write) an ESL newspaper with information on the school useful to a new student. Index the newspaper and use it as the basis for several "Where would I look for" exercises.

2. Have students make pocketbook-sized telephone directories for parents, filling in some useful information such as the school telephone number and numbers of friends and family.

Answers

Page 18

A.
1. Page 16
2. Page 51
3. Pages 31–41
4. Pages 19–23
5. Page 23
6. Page 6

B.
1. A and B
2. Page A2
3. Page A18
4. Page B8
5. Page B3

Page 20

A.
1. white pages
2. information
3. emergency
4. long distance
5. yellow pages

C.
1. Page 805
2. Page 465
3. Page 465
4. Page 359
5. Page 465

B.
2. Look in the yellow pages
3. Call information
4. Call long distance
5. Call emergency

Lesson 6	**Schedules, Page 21**

SKILL OBJECTIVE: Learning how to read various schedules

REINFORCEMENT ACTIVITIES:

In Content Classroom:

1. Within your content area there are probably already some materials dealing with the reading of schedules. If not, discuss the idea of budgeting time and have students write their own schedules. Use the results for class discussion.

2. Give students a hypothetical student's school schedule. Ask information-locating questions based on the schedule.

In ESL Classroom:

1. Bring newspaper, bus or train schedules to class and ask students questions based on the information.

2. Give students a copy of the school-year schedule. Ask them questions based on this, such as days off, test days, etc.

Answers

Page 22

A.
1. #900 E
2. 6:00 PM
3. 8:00 AM
4. #111 L
5. #900 E
6. 7:20 PM

B.
1. 6:30
2. 6:00
3. two
4. three

Page 24

A.

1. 6:00	5. Flt 210, Flt 208
2. 5	6. 7:00
3. 5:15	7. Omaha
4. 208	

B.

1. flight
2. arrive or (arrival)
3. depart or (departure)
4. on time
5. Estimated Time of Arrival

Lesson 7	**Diagrams, Page 25**

SKILL OBJECTIVE: Learning how to read box diagrams, line charts, bar charts and pie charts

REINFORCEMENT ACTIVITIES:

In Content Classroom:

1. Within your content area there are probably already some materials dealing with the reading of diagrams and charts. If not, use information from your subject area and ask students to devise diagrams and/or charts based on that information.

2. Use familiar information to have students draw diagrams and charts. This might include the school organization, school or classroom distribution of student types (boys/girls, various language groups, various ages).

In ESL Classroom:

1. If you are familiar with the methodology and in accord with it, you may want to teach students how to diagram simple sentences.

2. Use familiar information from students' personal lives for chart and diagram assignments. This might include a line chart of money earned or vocabulary learned, or a diagram of each person's monthly expenditures.

Answers

Page 26

A.

1. Vice President, Marketing
2. Plant Supervisor and Plant employees
3. Sales Manager
4. the President
5. the Plant Supervisor
6. two

B.

1. January and June
2. May
3. February
4. March
5. May
6. April

Page 28

A.

Food   Rent   Clothing   Transportation   Entertainment

B.

1. Food   2. Rent   3. Clothing   4. Transportation   5. Entertainment

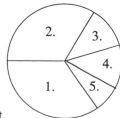

Lesson 8	Doing Homework/Taking Tests, Page 29

SKILL OBJECTIVE: Learning how to approach homework, learning how to use standard answer forms

REINFORCEMENT ACTIVITIES

In Content Classroom:

1. Much of your approach to this area will evolve from your own method of assigning homework. The more organized you are, the more organized you can expect all students to be.

2. Discuss homework responsibilities with student(s). You may want to require that homework be kept in a student folder or within a certain section of the student's notebook. Also make clear to student(s) what impact homework has on the course grade.

In ESL Classroom:

1. Make sure student notebooks are well-organized. If not, provide help in organizing by subject area.

2. Require student(s) periodically to show you homework from content area classes. This will help you plan your classwork and alert you to problem areas.

Answers

Page 30	Page 32
1. C	1. A
2. C	2. B
3. A	3. C
4. B	4. A
5. A	5. C
	6. A

Lesson 9	More About Taking Tests, Page 33

SKILL OBJECTIVE: Learning how to take matching and missing word(s) tests

REINFORCEMENT ACTIVITIES

In Content Classroom:

1. Assign student(s) the task of writing matching questions on recently covered information in your subject area. Choose the best questions and give an extra-credit quiz with them.

2. Assign student(s) the task of writing missing word(s) questions on recently covered information in your subject area. Choose the best questions and give an extra-credit quiz with them.

In ESL Classroom:

1. Have student(s) write matching questions on vocabulary or structures learned. Choose the best questions and give an extra-credit quiz with them.

2. Have student(s) write missing word(s) questions on known vocabulary or on a recently studied skill such as the use of reference material. Choose the best questions and give an extra-credit quiz with them.

Answers   **Page 34**

A.

1. 1. C   2. A   3. B

2. Lines are between

    A1 and B3

    A2 and B2

    A3 and B1

B.

Put the number of the correct answer on the line beside each place.

C.

1. B

2. C

3. A

Page 36

A.

1. 2. school   3. friends   4. talk   5. homework

2. 1. picture   2. watch

B.

1. Write in the missing word.

2. Write the missing words.

Lesson 10	**Studying for Tests/Memorizing, Page 37**

SKILL OBJECTIVE: Learning how to study and memorize

REINFORCEMENT ACTIVITIES

In Content Classroom:

1. Choose a recently studied unit and discuss with the students the specifics of how they should have studied for a unit test.

2. Using information from your text, follow the procedures for memorizing discussed in this lesson. Have student(s) practice the memorization orally with you.

In ESL Classroom:

1. Discuss with student(s) the differences among study skills for various subjects. Elicit from students any points that might need clarification on the subject of teacher expectations in content areas.

2. Give several exercises similar to the ones on Page 40. Encourage students to discover how else they might memorize.

Answers   **Page 38**

A.

1. C

2. C

3. B

B.

1. The book and anything else on the three parts of the United States government that I have.

2. Look at my papers and see what mistakes I made and why. Also read the chapter on addition of decimals.

3. Read Chapters One through Four again. Find the important information and remember it.

Page 40

A. 1. vocabulary words

their meanings

2. the three branches of government

what each does

3. the parts of the digestive system

what each does

B. 1. the inside of your hand between your fingers and your wrist *or* a tall, tropical tree

2. a pan

3. one side of a sheet of paper in a book *or* someone who calls people or runs errands

4. palm

Lesson 11	**Writing Reports—Composition Form/Book Reports, Page 41**

SKILL OBJECTIVE: Learning how to write compositions and book reports

REINFORCEMENT ACTIVITIES

In Content Classroom:

1. Discuss with student(s) any differences between the composition form that you require and that required by their other teachers. Give students exercises in taking information and putting it into composition form. Include indenting the first line of a paragraph.

2. Assign student(s) the task of writing a book report. If this does not seem feasible, ask that the book report form be used to report on a favorite TV show.

In ESL Classroom:

1. Ask student(s) to write a short report on some broad subject such as "My Favorite Country" or "My Favorite Friend." Require that reports be in the prescribed form.

2. Issue student(s) short books and require book reports. If age or English level is not high enough for this, read a short book to student(s) and ask for a simple book report on it.

Answers

Page 42　**A.**

Ms. Selden	John Thomas
Social Studies	March 6, 1993

The Industrial Revolution

B.

Mr. Jones	Susana Campo
English	(Date will vary.)

Life on the Mississippi
by
Mark Twain

C.

　　The Industrial Revolution was an exciting time in the United States. It was a revolution without guns. It made as big a difference in life, though, as a war with armies.

Page 44　**A.** The story　**B.** Check book report for essentials taught

Lesson 12	Information Reports, Page 45

SKILL OBJECTIVE: Learning how to get information for reports

REINFORCEMENT ACTIVITIES

In Content Classroom:

1. Assign a report to be written on something pertinent to your subject area, then follow the steps outlined on Page 45 with your student(s).

2. Require student(s) to follow the steps outlined on Page 47. Ask that notes be turned in with the completed report.

In ESL Classroom:

1. Take your student(s) to the school or local library and review where and how material can be found.

2. Ask your student(s) to write a report on a topic such as "My Homeland." Require that notes be turned in with the completed report.

Answers   Page 46   A.   1. B   2. E   3. B   4. A   5. C   6. A

Lesson 13	The Outline/The Summary, Page 49

SKILL OBJECTIVE: Learning how to organize and summarize information

REINFORCEMENT ACTIVITIES

In Content Classroom:

1. Using your text, assign student(s) the task of writing an outline of a particular chapter or section. Do this several times until you are sure student(s) understand(s) the outline form.

2. Using your text, assign student(s) the task of writing a summary of a particular chapter or section. Do this several times until you are sure student(s) understand(s) the summary requirements.

In ESL Classroom:

1. Assign student(s) the task of watching an informational television program and then outlining its main points. Discuss the differences that may arise among various students' perceptions of the program.

2. Assign student(s) the task of watching (or listening to) a 30-minute news program. Ask for a summary of the news presented. Discuss the differences that may arise.

Answers   Page 50

A. 1. 1. Geography
       2. History
       3. Way people live
       4. Politics

B. 1. Where goldfish come from
    2. How to take care of goldfish
    3. A story about goldfish

C. 1. Where the author was born
    2. How many books author wrote and their titles
    3. Prizes won by author
    4. Where author lives

Page 52

A. Summary C   **C.**   A. 2   B. 1   C. 3

| **Lesson 14** | **Reading Quickly for Information, Page 53** |

SKILL OBJECTIVES: Learning how to locate important words in reading and learning how to read groups of words together

REINFORCEMENT ACTIVITIES

In Content Classroom:

1. Give student(s) aural-oral practice by reading aloud short sentences from your text and asking which were the important words. Vary this by having student(s) read aloud to others.

2. Reproduce a page from your text. Have students go through it marking word groups to read together as in Exercise B, Page 56. Then have student(s) practice reading the word groups at one time.

In ESL Classroom:

1. Reproduce paragraphs from student texts. Have student(s) delete unimportant words. Discuss results.

2. Use a tachistoscope if available. If not, make flashcards with phrases. Have students practice reading a group of words at one time.

Answers

Page 54

A.

1. "You must help me clean the house," said my mother. (6)
2. Daniel Boone is one of the best known early American frontiersmen. (6)
3. Ranko stayed up late last night, watching an old movie on television about some gangsters. (8)
4. When we were walking to school yesterday, we saw an automobile accident on our street. (8)
5. Alice and Jean are good friends. (4)

B.

1. My class
   in Ms. Benson's room
   after three
   stayed
   noisy during Science

2. the window
   of a second-floor apartment in our building
   yesterday
   was broken
   by a terrible wind

3. Jack
   in the fast food place
   after school
   ordered hamburgers
   he was hungry

4. the manager
   during the second half
   sent for a doctor
   to see the injured player

Page 56

B. 1. Our teacher/took the class/to the library/to find some books.

2. The supermarket/was crowded with people/buying food/for the weekend.

3. "Thank you/for the birthday present,"/said Ms. Gates/to her son.

4. The Sunday newspaper/was full of stories/about the election.

5. The man at the employment office/said that/there weren't/any jobs.

6. The rock group/was giving a concert/in the park.

7. The passengers/listened to the pilot/and the stewardess.

8. Mr. Hyman said,/"You watch television/too much,/young man."

9. Many people believe/that world government/is possible/in the near future.

10. They ate roast beef,/rice,/vegetables and apple pie/for dinner.

Lesson 15	**What Information Is Important?, Page 57**

SKILL OBJECTIVE: Learning how to decide which information is important

REINFORCEMENT ACTIVITIES

In Content Classroom:

1. Using your text, help students find clues on what information is important (chapter and section headings, bold-type or italics print, lists). Have students look at The Table of Contents and Index as well as the body of the text.

2. Require student(s) to make an outline of at least one chapter in your text.

In ESL Classroom:

1. Use appropriate lessons from *Recognizing Details:* Book A, Lessons 7, 8, 13, 14, or, for the more advanced, Book B, Lessons 4, 5 (National Textbook Company).

2. Use other reading materials that are keyed to finding the important details in a short reading selection.

Answers

Page 58

A.   1. B   2. A   3. B   4. B

B.

Blanche and Henri went to a nice restaurant for dinner. ~~It was expensive, but the food was good.~~ ~~"You look lovely tonight," said Henry.~~ "Thank you," said Blanche, "I'm enjoying myself."

Page 60

A.

Page 33

3. Some tests ask you to put two parts of an answer together.

Page 35

4. Some tests have sentences with a missing word or words.

Page 37

5. When you study for a test, you must review information.

BOOK 3

Lesson 1	Dictionary Definitions, Page 1

SKILL OBJECTIVES: Understanding multiple definitions, synonyms and antonyms used in dictionary definitions

REINFORCEMENT ACTIVITIES

In Content Classroom:

1. Assign student(s) a list of words pertinent to your subject area. Using a textbook glossary or a dictionary, have student(s) copy definitions and then write sentences using each definition. In the case of a word with multiple meaning, discuss with student(s) how the appropriate meaning in a certain sentence can be determined by the context.

2. Give student(s) a list of adjectives appropriate to your subject area. Elicit antonyms for these adjectives. Discuss the selected antonyms and additional alternatives. (In Social Studies, for instance, *national* may have two antonyms: *local* and *international.)*

In ESL Classroom:

1. Discuss common homonyms and homophones with student(s). Assign a list appropriate to age and ESL level. Require student(s) to use words in sentences. From their sentences prepare a follow-up dictation for extra credit.

2. Choosing from known adjectives, prepare several exercises in which students match synonyms and antonyms.

Answers

Page 2

A.

2. Definition n. 3   4. Definition v. 4
3. Definition n. 1   5. Definition v. 1

B. and C.

Definitions will vary in specific wording depending on the dictionary used.

Page 4

A., B., C.

Definitions will vary in specific wording depending on the dictionary used.

Lesson 2	**Pronouncing Words/Accents, Page 5**

SKILL OBJECTIVE: Understanding key word examples and accents

REINFORCEMENT ACTIVITIES

In Content Classroom:

1. To give aural-oral reinforcement to these lessons, you may want to teach direct pronunciation of key words in a dictionary available to the students. Model pronunciation twice, then ask the students to repeat the word, concentrating on the variation of the vowel sound.

2. You may, depending on your subject and the grade level of your students, use this opportunity to direct their attention to footnotes, since this information is as much ignored as key words.

In ESL Classroom:

1. Teach a number of lessons in aural-oral discrimination through vowel contrast in minimal pairs such as *pat-pot, pan-pen*. Relate pronunciation of vowels to dictionary key words.

2. Teach several lessons in word stresses. You may also want to relate this to the previous lesson with words that change stress according to meaning.

Answers

Page 6

1. cup, about
2. ate, late
3. met, get, order, more
4. cup, about, boy, oil
5. sit, is
6. sit, is
7. ice, my
8. equal, easy
9. order, more
10. cup, about, term, bird
11. cup, about
12. top, stop, order, more
13. order, more
14. rule, food, sit, is
15. equal, easy
16. open, coat
17. jar, far, term, bird
18. equal, easy
19. rule, food
20. ate, late

Page 8

A.

2. 1
3. 1
4. 1
5. 2
6. 1
7. 2
8. 1
9. 2
10. 1
11. 1
12. 1

B.

2. wel come	1
3. gas o line	3
4. prop er ty	1
5. Sat ur day	1
6. tel e phone	1
7. Oc to ber	2
8. de light ful	2
9. paint ing	1
10. gi raffe	2

Lesson 3	**Putting Facts Together/Putting Ideas Together, Page 9**

SKILL OBJECTIVE: Practicing the organization of information into categories

REINFORCEMENT ACTIVITIES

In Content Classroom:

1. Give student(s) a list of categories appropriate to your subject area. In a timed contest, ask the student(s) to fill in each category with words that they know. Compare lists and award extra credit for the best.

2. Using the categories listed on Page 11, ask students to use one chapter or section of your text and to organize material into the given categories. Compare results and give extra credit for the best.

In ESL Classroom:

1. Give student(s) a list of words to be remembered after 5 minutes' study. Test them. Then give student(s) the same list grouped in categories. After 1 minute, check their recall.

2. If available play a game like Concentration©, urging students to categorize for better memory.

Answers

Page 10

A.

SPORTS	FOOD	PEOPLE
football	candy	woman
team	eggs	team
player	milk	boy
umpire	cake	player
soccer		umpire
referee		referee

B.

1. furniture
2. earning money
3. times
4. colors
5. entertainment
6. changing jobs
7. fast food
8. going to the doctor
9. supermarket food
10. going to the post office

Page 12

A.

2. when	7. where
3. where	8. how
4. where	9. when
5. when	10. where
6. how	

B.

2. thing	7. white
3. love	8. sing
4. run	9. doctor
5. Lester	10. Tuesday
6. teacher	

Lesson 4	**Understanding Relationships—Synonyms/Numbers, Page 13**

SKILL OBJECTIVE: Understanding analogies of synonyms and numbers

REINFORCEMENT ACTIVITIES

In Content Classroom:

1. Since the material in this lesson is concerned with word and number relationships, your approach to the material will be governed by your own subject matter. You may want to present additional exercises on synonyms or, if you are a Math teacher, on number analogies.

2. Many students find it useful to construct their own analogies with synonyms or numbers. Assign this task and then use the results for further practice with the students.

In ESL Classroom:

1. Have students develop synonym lists of known vocabulary. Use these lists in preparing additional analogy exercises for them.

2. Expand student understanding of number analogies with the variant of number progressions. This can be, for example, such a progression as 1,5,3,9,7 (+4, -2) or more complicated relationships.

Answers

Page 14		Page 16	
A.	**B.**	**A.**	**B.**
1. B	1. B	1. A	1. A
2. A	2. A	2. B	2. B
3. B	3. C	3. C	3. C
4. C	4. A	4. A	4. A
5. C	5. B	5. B	5. C
6. A	6. C	6. A	6. A
7. B	7. B	7. C	7. B
8. C	8. A	8. C	8. A
9. B	9. A	9. B	9. B
10. B	10. C	10. A	10. A
11. C			

Lesson 5	**Understanding Relationships—Antonyms/Part to Whole, Page 17**

SKILL OBJECTIVE: Understanding analogies of antonyms and part to whole

REINFORCEMENT ACTIVITIES

In Content Classroom:

1. Since this and succeeding lessons are "thinking skills" lessons, you may want to discuss with students the motivations for understanding relationships, and using language to help us think.

2. Part-to-whole relationships are sometimes difficult to grasp. Helpful exercises are those based on close-up pictures of various surfaces, simple jigsaw puzzles or even the old standby of "Hangman."

In ESL Classroom:

1. Have students develop antonym lists of known vocabulary. Use these lists in preparing additional analogy exercises for them.

2. If students have difficulty understanding part-to-whole analogies, give them a list of words to be placed in a limited number of categories. Use this as a basis for making part-to-whole analogy exercises as on Page 20.

Answers

	Page 18			Page 20	
	A.	**B.**		**A.**	**B.**
1.	A	1. B		1. A	1. B
2.	B	2. B		2. B	2. A
3.	B	3. A		3. A	3. B
4.	C	4. A		4. C	4. C
5.	A	5. C		5. B	5. A
6.	A	6. A		6. A	6. A
7.	C	7. B		7. C	7. A
8.	B	8. A		8. B	8. C
9.	A	9. A		9. A	9. C
10.	C	10. C		10. C	10. A
11.	A				11. C

Lesson 6	**What Does It Mean?/Facts That Mean the Same, Page 21**

SKILL OBJECTIVE: Synthesizing and concluding from facts

REINFORCEMENT ACTIVITIES

In Content Classroom:

1. Give students material appropriate to your course that contains unstated information. Discuss how facts put together can give us a conclusion that is not given in words.

2. Give students statements that can be illustrated by examples. Then have students write the examples to give the information in an unstated way.

In ESL Classroom:

1. Give students a series of paired sentences that can be combined into one, particularly by using dependent clauses. Discuss how meaning can be changed if one is not careful. Do several exercises of this type organized around a particular type of dependent clause such as *When* clauses.

2. Give students a list of incomplete facts and ask them to combine the information into as few sentences as possible. Discuss different responses and their validity.

Answers

Page 22			Page 24			
A.		**B.**	**A.**		**B.**	
1. B		1. B	1. C		1. S	
2. C		2. C	2. A		2. D	
3. B		3. A	3. E		3. S	
4. A			4. B		4. S	
5. B			5. D		5. S	
			6. G			
			7. F			

Lesson 7	**What Sentence Will Come Next?/What Happens Next?, Page 25**

SKILL OBJECTIVES: Learning to predict next sentence or sentences

REINFORCEMENT ACTIVITIES

In Content Classroom:

1. Plan a series of exercises to relate prediction to your own subject area. In Math this could be predicting the question that will be asked in a number problem. In Science it could be predicting the outcome of an experiment. In Social Studies it could be predicting the information to be given in a chapter based on the beginning paragraph(s).

2. Assign students to write prediction problems with multiple choice answers, similar to the exercises suggested in number 1 above. Use the best for class practice and discussion.

In ESL Classroom:

1. Ask students to write prediction exercises similar to the ones in this lesson. Use the best for class practice and discussion.

2. Read the beginning of a short story, such as O. Henry's "Gift of the Magi," and ask student(s) to write the ending.

Answers

Page 26   1. A   2. B   3. C   4. C

Page 28   1. B   2. A   3. A   4. A

Lesson 8	Predicting the End, Page 29

SKILL OBJECTIVE: Learning to predict the end of factual or fictional writing

REINFORCEMENT ACTIVITIES

In Content Classroom:

1. Using any visual materials available to you from magazine pictures to filmstrips, present students with a situation. Ask them to write two or three sentences about how the situation might be resolved. Discuss the different solutions.

2. Using the facts of a recent discovery in your field, write a brief paragraph on events leading up to that discovery. Ask students to predict what the discovery was, then discuss their right (and wrong) conclusions.

In ESL Classroom:

1. If available, use suggested activities based on Lessons 7 and 8 Book C in *Identifying Main Ideas* and *Recognizing Details* (National Textbook Company, 1990).

2. Tell the students the story of "The Lady or the Tiger." Ask them to write an end to the story. Discuss the logic of the endings they have chosen.

Answers

Page 30

Suggested predictions are not the only correct answers. Teacher judgment should be used here.

1. It will probably end by talking about his death.

2. It will probably end by saying something about John Hustin going back to work after his vacation.

3. It will probably end by Ari saying that he wants to speak both of his languages better.

4. Trude will probably do her homework.

Page 32

1. This story will probably end with Will and the girl becoming friends.

2. This story will probably end with Jimmy and his friends talking to whoever was inside the UFO.

3. This story will probably end with the doctor following the lawyer's advice.

4. This story will probably end with Jane and the president going to dinner together.

Lesson 9	Deciding on the Page, Page 33

SKILL OBJECTIVE: Learning how to judge reading material for facts

REINFORCEMENT ACTIVITIES

In Content Classroom:

1. Ask students to bring magazine or newspaper advertisements to class. Use these as a basis for oral discussion of fact vs. opinion.

2. Using your text, assign students the task of taking fact statements from a particular page or chapter and turning them into opinions by using the verbs "think" or "feel."

In ESL Classroom:

1. If available, use Lesson 2, Book C of *Recognizing Details* (National Textbook Company, 1990) to reinforce understanding of fact and opinion.

2. Assign students the task of changing sentences on Page 34 from fact to opinion or from opinion to fact.

Answers

Page 34

A. Fact sentences are 2, 3, 4, 5, 7, 9, 10.

B. Opinion sentences are 1, 5, 7, 9, 10.

Page 36

1. Fact. Why? because there is no opinion involved.

2. Fact. Why? because maps can demonstrate that this is true.

3. Fact. Why? because there is no opinion involved.

4. Opinion and Fact. Why? The word "like" shows that it is an opinion. The last part of the sentence is true from preceding information.

5. Opinion. Why? The word "think" shows that it is an opinion.

6. Opinion. Why? The word "wise" cannot be proved simply because they make a statement that agrees with the writer.

7. Opinion and Fact. "My heart" shows that the first part is opinion. The last part is demonstrably true.

Lesson 10	Why and What/What and Why, Page 37

SKILL OBJECTIVE: Learning how to determine cause and effect in reading

REINFORCEMENT ACTIVITIES

In Content Classroom:

1. Devise a series of logic exercises appropriate to your discipline. Various aspects of Math lend themselves well to this. In Social Studies, action-result classifications can be based on historical or geographical events. In Science, experiments are prime examples of cause/effect.

2. Give students a list of effects related to your subject. Ask them to supply the cause or causes.

In ESL Classroom:

1. Give students a list of clauses beginning with *because*. Ask them to supply the rest of the sentence showing the effect of what happened.

2. Assign students the task of completing the sentences in A, Page 40. In addition, provide your own exercise for combining sentences as in B, Page 38.

Answers

Page 38

A. There may be alternative logical answers.

1. cold	6. buses
2. early	7. tired
3. hurt	8. fell
4. people	9. winning
5. big	10. money

B.

1. We were late getting home today because there were many cars on the road.

2. Because the player hit a home run, the fans stood up and cheered.

3. Because Franz loves Ilse, he asked her to marry him.

4. Because the weather was getting colder, the birds flew South.

5. We bought chicken because the beef was too expensive.

Page 40

A.

1. E	7. C
2. C	8. E
3. C	9. C
4. E	10. E
5. E	
6. C	

B. Accept any logical answers.

1. we called the fire department.

2. because she wanted to talk about the class dance.

3. because she wanted to talk to me.

4. I didn't wait.

5. because the teacher had not come.

6. because it was a nice day.

7. because I wanted to save money.

Lesson 11	**Understanding the Meaning, Page 41**

SKILL OBJECTIVE: Understanding the implications in reading

REINFORCEMENT ACTIVITIES

In Content Classroom:

1. Review the Fact and Opinion lesson with students. Discuss examples of materials pertinent to your subject which state an opinion without cue words such as *think* or *feel*.

2. Ask students to bring to class and discuss a paragraph that shows opinion. A good source is the local newspaper's editorial page.

In ESL Classroom:

1. If available, use Lessons 10 and 11 in *Recognizing Details*. Discuss with students how they understood the unstated details.

2. Give students an assignment of writing short paragraphs on a given opinion. Students must not actually state the opinion but prove it through details.

Answers	Page 42	1. B		Page 44	1. A	3. C
		2. C			2. C	4. B
		3. B				

Lesson 12   **Reading about Emotions/Facts in Advertising, Page 45**

SKILL OBJECTIVE: Understanding implications of mood writing and of advertising

REINFORCEMENT ACTIVITIES

In Content Classroom:

1. Assign students the task of writing down the words of a television commercial they like. Ask each student to present his/her commercial in class and then have students discuss what kind of mood is presented.

2. Show students an evocative picture and discuss its mood with them. Assign the task of writing a paragraph about the picture without using the particular mood word.

In ESL Classroom:

1. If available, use Lessons 12 and 13, Book C in *Recognizing Details*. Discuss the moods the various paragraphs evoke.

2. Have students bring magazine and newspaper ads to class. Discuss with them what mood each is designed to evoke.

Answers

Page 46	A.	B.	Page 48	A.	B.
	1. B	1. C		1. No	1. No
	2. C	2. C		2. Yes	2. No
	3. D			3. No	3. No
	4. A			4. No	4. No
	5. E			5. No	5. No
				6. No	6. No

Lesson 13   **The Language of Algebra/Science Experiments, Page 49**

VOCABULARY

Algebra:

numeral	phrase
constant	expression
variable	

Science Experiments:

Bunsen burner	stain	emulsion
petri dish	slide	sterile
test tube	solution	

REINFORCEMENT ACTIVITIES

In Content Classroom:

1. In the Algebra classroom, find examples of the concepts taught in the textbook. Alternatively, have students find examples. Discuss these examples to be sure that understanding is complete.

2. In the science classroom, present the actual materials for the vocabulary taught. If possible, assign students an experiment to write up that includes the vocabulary.

In ESL Classroom:	1.	As much as possible, work with examples from the student textbooks to practice use of vocabulary taught.	
	2.	Ask students to write short paragraphs explaining the vocabulary.	

Answers **Page 50**

A.
1. numeral
2. variable
3. numerical phrase
4. algebraic phrase
5. not correct
6. correct
7. variable
8. variable

B.
1. variable
2. algebraic expression
3. numerical phrase
4. numeral
5. the symbol ×

Page 52

A.
1. petri dish
2. Bunsen burner
3. solution
4. test tube
5. emulsion
6. slide

B.
1. test tube
2. Bunsen burner
3. petri dish
4. slide

Lesson 14	**Special Computer Vocabulary, Page 53**

VOCABULARY

cursor	function	input	modem	output	prompt
data	graphics	menu	mouse	pen	

REINFORCEMENT ACTIVITIES

In Content Classroom:
1. In the Computer room, present the actual materials for the vocabulary taught. If possible, ask students to write a paragraph using the vocabulary that explains how to use the computer.
2. Ask students to give oral presentations using computers to explain the vocabulary.

In ESL Classroom:
1. Ask students to write short paragraphs to explain the vocabulary words.
2. Have students give an oral talk on computer use that incorporates the vocabulary.

Answers   **Page 54**   **A.**   **B.**

1. function keys   1. mouse
2. mouse   2. cursor
3. menu   3. function keys
4. cursor   4. menu
                    5. pen

Page 56   **A.**   **B.**

1. data   1. input
2. prompt   2. output
3. output   3. graphics
4. modem   4. prompt
5. input   5. modem
6. graphics   6. data

Lesson 15	**Special Meanings, Page 57**

SKILL OBJECTIVE: Understanding and interpreting figurative and exaggerated comparisons

REINFORCEMENT ACTIVITIES

In Content Classroom:

1. According to your subject area, use your text or other pertinent materials that employ figurative language. Ask students to identify the phrases or groups of words and tell what they mean.

2. Ask students to bring to class a joke or cartoon that they don't understand. Discuss its meaning with them.

In ESL Classroom:

1. Introduce students to simple lyric poetry and discuss how the poet presents meaning through figurative language. Have students write simple couplets or quatrains using figurative language.

2. Teach the difference between simile and metaphor. Have students write humorous comparisons in each form.

Answers   **Page 58**   **A.**   **B.**

1. C   5. A   1. B   5. C
2. B   6. B   2. A   6. B
3. A   7. B   3. C   7. A
4. B   8. B   4. B   8. B

Page 60   Answers will vary.

VOCABULARY BY CONTENT AREA

Specialized Vocabulary—General School

BOOK 1

Lesson 1

Answer the question.
Close your book.
Copy the work.
Open your book.
Please be quiet.
Put away your book.
Raise your hand.
Read.
Sit down.
Stand up.
Take out your book.

Lesson 2

Art
Computer
English
Gym
Math/Mathematics
Music
Science
Social Studies

Specialized Vocabulary—Social Studies

BOOK 1

Lesson 3

book
city
country
land
map
nation
ocean
people
river
world

Lesson 9

bridge
building
direction
east
highway
lake
north
road
south
west

Lesson 13

Mid-Atlantic
Midwestern
Northeastern
Southern
Southwestern
states
Western

Specialized Vocabulary—Math

BOOK 1

Lesson 4

add
addition
divide
division
multiplication
multiply
number
problem
subtract
subtraction

Lesson 10

decimal
equal
fraction
greater than
less than
minus
percent
plus
total
whole

BOOK 3

Lesson 13

constant
expression
numeral
phrase
variable

Specialized Vocabulary—Science

BOOK 1

BOOK 3

Lesson 5	Lesson 11	Lesson 13
animal	cold	Bunsen burner
bird	down	emulsion
fish	flower	petri dish
microscope	grow	slide
moon	hot	solution
plant	rain	stain
star	season	sterile
sun	temperature	test tube
telescope	up	
tree	weather	

Specialized Vocabulary—Computer

BOOK 1

BOOK 3

Lesson 7

boot	keyboard
disk	printer
disk drive	program
display	screen
floppy disk	software
hardware	

Lesson 14

cursor	modem
data	mouse
function	output
graphics	pen
input	prompt
menu	

Specialized Vocabulary—Art

BOOK 1

Lesson 8

color
crayon
draw
paint
picture

Specialized Vocabulary— Music

BOOK 1

Lesson 8

piano
play
tape
sing
song

Answer Keys for the Tests

BOOK 1

Math Learning
(20 Points)

1. numbers
2. subtract
3. add
4. multiplication
5. division
6. minus
7. equal
8. plus
9. greater than
10. total
11. percent
12. fraction
13. 13 + 12 = 25 students
14. 1 + 1 + 7 = 9 people
15. 25 − 15 = 10 men teachers
16. 8 − 4 = 4 other rooms
17. 2 × 12 = 24 books
18. 25 × 5 = 125 students
19. 18 ÷ 3 = 6 students
20. 30 ÷ 3 = 10 stops

Social Studies Learning
(20 Points)

1. country
2. nation
3. world
4. city
5. river
6. people
7. ocean
8. west
9. east
10. south
11. highway
12. bridge
13. building
14. lake
15. Arizona, Colorado, Nevada, Oklahoma, Texas, Utah
16. California, Idaho, Montana, Oregon, Washington, Wyoming
17. Connecticut, Maine, Massachusetts, New Hampshire, New Jersey, New York, Pennsylvania, Rhode Island, Vermont
18. Illinois, Indiana, Iowa, Kansas, Michigan, Minnesota, Missouri, Nebraska, North Dakota, South Dakota
19. Delaware, Maryland, North Carolina, South Carolina, Virginia, West Virginia
20. Alabama, Arkansas, Florida, Georgia, Kentucky, Louisiana, Mississippi, Tennessee

Science Learning
(20 Points)

1. plants
2. fish
3. animals
4. trees
5. birds
6. telescope
7. moon
8. microscope
9. sun
10. stars
11. flower
12. seasons
13. rain
14. weather
15. grow
16. cold
17. temperature
18. down
19. hot
20. up

English Learning
(20 Points)

1. listen
2. words
3. talk
4. language
5. speak
6. write
7. read
8. composition
9. paragraph
10. sentence
11. letters
12. period
13. capital
14. small
15. punctuation
16. letter
17. date
18. signature
19. question mark
20. comma

Classroom and Minor Subject Learning
(20 Points)

1. c
2. a
3. c
4. a
5. b
6. Math
7. Social Studies
8. Science
9. English
10. Gym
11. hardware
12. screen
13. program
14. software
15. keyboard
16. paint
17. colors
18. tapes
19. piano
20. sing

BOOK 2   LESSONS 1–7

Alphabetical Order
(20 Points)

1. good, nice
2. apple, baby
3. six, twenty
4. love, more
5. time, up
6. English, Math, Social Studies
7. Art, Gym, Music
8. divide, multiply, subtract
9. correct, right, wrong
10. moon, sun, telescope
11. late, like
12. sew, star
13. clean, cook
14. sing, song
15. piano, play
16. stand, stop
17. both, boy
18. won't, world
19. thing, think
20. find, fine

II.   The Library and Reference Books
(20 Points)

A.   THE LIBRARY
1. card catalog
2. author
3. title
4. alphabetical order
5. nonfiction
6. biography
7. encyclopedia
8. fiction
9. dictionary
10. reference

B.   THE DICTIONARY
1. spare
2. of or belonging to Spain
3. space
4. spark
5. distance or area between or within things

C.   THE ENCYCLOPEDIA
1. 4
2. 1
3. 5
4. 4
5. 1

III.   Parts of Books
(20 Points)

A.   THE TABLE OF CONTENTS
1. 91
2. 3
3. 1
4. 5
5. 2, 3
6. 4
7. 5
8. 2
9. 3
10. 6

B.   THE INDEX
1. 5, 7
2. 13, 15, 37, 39, 53–60
3. 6
4. 31
5. 29
6. 27
7. 21, 23, 45, 47
8. 4
9. 27
10. 8

IV.   Life Reference Books
(20 Points)

A.   THE NEWSPAPER INDEX
1. pp. 12–16
2. p. 51
3. p. 24
4. pp. 19–23
5. p. 16

B.   THE TELEPHONE DIRECTORY
1. a
2. c
3. b
4. b
5. a

V.   Schedules and Diagrams
(20 Points)

A.   SCHEDULES
(10 Points)

1. 6:15
2. 3
3. San Antonio
4. 5
5. #5, #10

B.   DIAGRAMS
(10 Points)

1. Principal
2. Ms. B and Mr. A
3. Mr. A
4. Mr. A
5. Ms. B

BOOK 2   LESSONS 8–15

I.   Test Taking
(15 Points)

A. 1. a
2. a
3. b
4. b
5. b

B. 1. sentences
2. missing
3. words
4. write
5. test

C. Answers will vary.

II.   Writing Reports
(20 Points)

A.   REPORT FORM
(10 Points)

1. Ms. Gordon   John Miller
Science   February 4, 1992
The Peaceful Use of Atomic Power

2. Answers will vary.

B.   LOCATING INFORMATION FOR A REPORT
(10 Points)

1. d
2. a
3. c
4. b
5. f
6. e
7. f
8. b
9. c
10. b

III. The Outline
(20 Points)

A. (10 Points)

1. Where she was born
2. Where she went to school
3. What she did later
4. When she died
5. Why we remember her

B. (10 Points)

1.
  1. Picasso was born in Spain.
  2. He lived in France most of his life.
  3. His most famous painting is *Guernica.*
  4. He did many things besides painting in his later life.

2. Answers will vary

IV. The Summary
(20 Points)

A. (10 Points)

1. C
2. C

B. (10 Points)

A. 3
B. 5
C. 1
D. 2
E. 4

V. Judging Important Information
(20 Points)

A. (10 Points)
1. b
2. c
3. c
4. b
5. c

B. (10 Points)
The sky became as black as night. The wind grew stronger and stronger. My mother said, "Bring the dog and the cat inside. This is going to be bad." Soon the rain came. *(A line should be drawn through these sentences.)*

BOOK 3 LESSONS 1–8

I. Dictionary Skills
(30 Points)

A. UNDERSTANDING DEFINITIONS
(16 Points)

1. adj. 1
2. v. 3
3. n.
4. adj. 2
5. v. 2
6. v. 1
7. n.
8. adj. 2

B. PRONUNCIATION
(14 Points)

1. cup, about
2. sit, is
3. order, more
4. equal, easy
5. open, coat
6. ate, late
7. rule, food

II. Categorizing
(20 Points)

A. (10 Points)

PEOPLE: man, girl, teacher
COLORS: blue, red, white, yellow
PLACES: school, apartment, building

B. (10 Points)

1. months
2. transportation
3. numbers
4. food
5. emergencies
6. sports
7. time
8. jobs
9. entertainment
10. music

III. Analogies
(40 Points)

A. SYNONYMS
(10 Points)

1. b
2. a
3. b
4. c
5. a

B. ANTONYMS
(10 Points)

1. c
2. b
3. a
4. b
5. b

C. NUMBERS
(10 Points)

1. b
2. a
3. a
4. c
5. b

D. PART TO WHOLE
(10 Points)

1. a
2. c
3. b
4. a
5. a

IV. Synthesizing and Concluding
(10 Points)

1. c
2. c
3. b
4. b
5. c

V. Predicting
(20 Points)

A. NEXT SENTENCE
(10 Points)

1. a
2. c
3. b
4. a
5. a

B. **PREDICTING THE END OF WRITING**
(10 Points)

1. c
2. a
3. b
4. a
5. a

BOOK 3   LESSONS 9–15

I. **Facts and Opinions**
(20 Points)

1. O
2. F
3. O
4. F
5. F
6. O
7. F
8. F
9. O
10. F

II. **Cause and Effect**
(20 Points)

1. C
2. E
3. E
4. C
5. E
6. E
7. E
8. C
9. C
10. E

III. **Hidden Meaning**
(20 Points)

1. b
2. a
3. c
4. b

IV. **Mood, Figurative Meaning**
(20 Points)

A. **MOOD**
(10 Points)

1. b
2. c
3. b

1. b
2. c

B. **FIGURATIVE MEANING**
(10 Points)

1. a
2. a
3. c
4. b
5. c